complete
self help
for your
nerves

DR CLAIRE WEEKES

HarperCollins*Publishers*

HarperCollins*Publishers*

First published in Australia in 1962 by Angus & Robertson Publishers
This edition published in 2008
by HarperCollins*Publishers* Australia Pty Limited
ABN 36 009 913 517
harpercollins.com.au

Copyright © Claire Weekes 2008, 1997, 1984, 1962

The right of Claire Weekes to be identified as the author of this
work has been asserted under the *Copyright Amendment
(Moral Rights) Act 2000.*

This work is copyright. Apart from any use as permitted under the
Copyright Act 1968, no part may be reproduced, copied, scanned, stored
in a retrieval system, recorded, or transmitted, in any form or by any
means, without the prior written permission of the publisher.

HarperCollins*Publishers*
Level 13, 201 Elizabeth Street, Sydney NSW 2000, Australia
Unit D, 63 Apollo Drive, Rosedale, Auckland 0632, New Zealand
A 53, Sector 57, Noida, UP, India
1 London Bridge Street, London SE1 9GF, United Kingdom
2 Bloor Street East, 20th floor, Toronto, Ontario M4W 1A8, Canada
195 Broadway NY, NY 10007, United States of America

National Library of Australia Cataloguing-in-Publication data:

Weekes, Claire.
    Complete self-help for your nerves / author, Dr Claire Weekes.
    Revised ed.
    Pymble, N.S.W. : HarperCollins, 2008.
    ISBN: 9780732287078 (pbk.)
    Stress (Psychology) – Popular works.
    Self-care, Health.
    Panic disorders – Popular works.
    Neuroses – Popular works.
616.852068

Cover and internal design by Darren Holt
Cover image: image # 200548850-001, courtesy of Getty Images
Typeset in 11/17pt Sabon by Kirby Jones
Printed and bound in Australia by McPherson's Printing Group
70gsm Classic used by HarperCollins*Publishers* is a natural, recyclable product made from
wood grown in sustainable forests. The manufacturing processes conform to the
environmental regulations in the country of origin, Finland.

Dedicated with esteem to the many whose courage has helped to make this book

Contents

1. The power within you

If you are reading this book because you are having a nervous breakdown or because your nerves are 'in a bad way', you are the very person for whom it has been written and I shall therefore talk directly to you as if you were sitting beside me.

I shall show clearly and simply, and yet with all necessary detail, just how a nervous breakdown begins and develops and how it can be cured. RECOVERY IS DEFINITELY ACHIEVABLE IF YOU FOLLOW THE ADVICE GIVEN HERE. This will take perseverance and some courage. You may notice that I have not asked for patience. Nervously sick people are rarely patient, because sick nerves are usually agitated nerves – that is one reason why they become bewildered by them. To wait patiently in a queue can be almost intolerable misery for such people. However, there is a substitute for patience and this I shall present to you later.

It will not be difficult for you to read this book: it is about you and your nerves, and for this reason you will read it with interest, whereas to read an ordinary book or newspaper may seem an impossibility, or, should you succeed, may leave you more distressed than when you began.

I used the word 'cure' and this may surprise you, because it implies an illness and you may think of yourself as more bewildered than ill – lost in a maze trying to find your way back to the person you used to be. On the other hand, you may be so depressed and exhausted that you may readily agree that you are ill. Either way, 'illness' and 'cure' are clear and convenient labels for 'the way you feel now' and 'the way you would like to feel'.

Whether or not you consider yourself ill, more than anything else you want to be yourself again. You probably look at others in the street and wonder why you can't be like them. What is this 'terrible thing' that has happened to you? What is the meaning of these terrifying feelings?

Such feelings may have possessed you for a long time, even for years. Indeed, you may have reached a point of such desperate suffering that you could be thinking of suicide, or may even have attempted it. And yet, however deeply involved you may be in nervous breakdown, it is possible to recover and enjoy life again. I emphasise, however deeply involved.

The guidance you need is in this book. The perseverance and courage you can, with help, find within yourself. The strength to recover is within you, once you are shown the way. I assure you of this.

Each of us has unsuspected power to accomplish what we demand of ourselves, if we care to search for it. You are no exception. You can find it if you make up your mind to, however great a coward you may think yourself at this moment. I have no illusions about you: I am not writing this book for the rare brave people, but for you, probably a sick, suffering, ordinary human being with no more courage than the rest of us, but – and this is the important thing – with the same unplumbed, unsuspected power in reserve as the rest of us. It is possible that you may be aware of such power but may feel, because of your nervous condition, unable to release it. This book will help you find this power, and show you how to release and use it.

2. Nervous fatigue

Understanding nervous fatigue is the key to understanding the baffling experiences that make recovery from nervous illness so elusive – within grasp one minute, gone the next. Understanding is the fore-runner of cure.

Nervous fatigue can show itself as one, or more, of four fatigues: muscular, emotional, mental and a kind of fatigue of the spirit, and these often develop in this order. (I will discuss them in this order in the following four chapters.)

That sounds straightforward enough, yet few people recognise these fatigues in themselves because their development has been so gradual, so insidious. And yet, this development follows a consistent pattern which is the basis of so much nervous suffering.

Indeed, recognising fatigue as an important part of their illness can bring such relief to so many, their subsequent recovery can be straightforward and simple. I said simple. I did not say easy.

At this moment, while you read this, you may be bewildered by what is happening to you. Perhaps the task of facing today, tomorrow, seems too much for your exhausted body to attempt, too much for your tired mind to think about. And yet it may be only a few months since you could have done that, and much more, so easily.

You may have reached the stage where you feel you would rather close your eyes and never open them again than have to open them tomorrow. All this may be so unlike your old self – indeed may seem to be a reversal of that former self – that your bewilderment may be extreme.

When I explain to some bewildered, nervously ill people that their suffering is based on nervous fatigue, they are at first dubious that such strange, disturbing symptoms as theirs, such utter exhaustion, could have such an apparently simple cause. However, when convinced, being nervously fatigued seems less frightening than the 'mental' illness they were beginning to suspect was theirs. Their picture of mental illness has so many dark, mysterious places.

The difference between nervous fatigue and nervous illness must be explained. A person can suffer from one, or all, of the four fatigues – muscular, emotional, mental and 'spiritual' – and still, in my opinion, not be nervously ill. It is only when he becomes *afraid of the effects* of fatigue and allows this fear to interfere with his life, that I say he has passed from being nervously fatigued to being nervously ill.

Of course there are many different kinds of nervous illness. I am concerned mainly with the simplest and most common kind: the anxiety state.

Anxiety is closely related to fear. The difference between them is one of timing as well as of intensity. For instance, in an acute emergency – such as facing an immediate danger –

we would say we were afraid, whereas when contemplating a threatening future even we would say we were anxious rather than afraid.

The term 'anxious' comes from the Latin *anxius* meaning being upset about some future uncertain happening. So, literally, being in an anxiety *state* should mean being in a condition of prolonged anxiety. However, in practice, a person in an anxiety state is both anxious and afraid and is very often particularly afraid of his nervous symptoms.

I say 'particularly afraid of his symptoms' because there are two main types of anxiety state. In the first, the original stress has passed and is no longer responsible for the illness. The sufferer is now concerned with fear of the symptoms this original stress brought. He is afraid of the state he is in, caught in a maze of fear from which he cannot free himself. So his continuing anxiety state is based on fear of symptoms.

In the second type, the sufferer is more concerned with some problem, or problems, that may have caused his illness and is not cured until this, or these, are resolved. Peace of mind about his problems is usually essential for his cure.

In my practice the vast majority of people were afraid of their nervous symptoms and often also of the strange experiences stress brought, and in this book I am mainly concerned with them. However, my teaching about understanding nervous fatigue also helps people with a specific problem, or problems (even those with a subconscious cause of illness) – it gives them an understanding of their symptoms and experiences, which at least clears some bewilderment and so opens the way to recovery.

Hypochondria In my opinion, few nervously ill people are true hypochondriacs. They are simply people who are tired of being ill and are so sensitised, they feel they can't bear the extra strain of worrying about new physical symptoms. They should not be ashamed if they feel they need to visit their doctor frequently, to get relief from worry. They should explain to their doctor that in their present state they cannot avoid noticing every new symptom that appears; that their nerves are reacting in an exaggerated way and they need the peace they hope his explanation will bring. They are not true hypochondriacs.

As mentioned earlier, as long as a nervously fatigued person is not unduly anxious about, or afraid of, his condition, he is not, in my opinion, in an anxiety state, not nervously ill.

Regardless of whether a person is nervously ill or merely nervously fatigued, he will benefit from understanding the four fatigues. Even those people who have never suffered from nervous fatigue can be protected from it by understanding it.

So let me guide you, as I have guided so many, to an understanding of nervous fatigue and to recovery from any existing nervous illness.

3. Muscular fatigue

THE FIRST FATIGUE

Ordinary muscular fatigue is easy to recognise. It may come after strenuous exercise, when it's good to relax – especially in a hot bath – and enjoy the aching muscles that speak so satisfyingly of achievement. However, the muscular fatigue that comes with nervous fatigue is not enjoyable. It comes, not from the extra use of muscles, but from their abuse – from subjecting them to too constant and too severe tension.

Strenuous sport while depleted? I have never met a depleted person who wanted to play strenuous sport. However, I have seen some young people who thought they were too weak to leave the beds on which they had been lying for years, play tennis after only a few weeks of the right treatment.

One man, more or less confined to bed for nine years, said he felt so ill he hadn't the strength to read my book; a friend read it to him. And yet, after

listening to these readings and then practising
walking with golfsticks as crutches, he was playing
tennis within six weeks. His story was published in
the *New York Times Magazine* around Christmas
1977. One finds strength quicker when active than
when lying on the couch waiting for it to come.

I encourage patients to be active, but before
I would advise strenuous sport I would need to
examine the adventurer. Swimming I advise
because it need not be strenuous and if in salt
water is especially soothing to those trying to
withdraw from drug therapy. It brings its own
sedation.

Also, during the agitation that can accompany drug
withdrawal, exercises help 'let off steam', and I
recommend them.

Resting muscles are usually in a condition called
tone, which is a state balanced between relaxation and
contraction; in this way, they are kept ready for use. Tone is
maintained by reflex nervous arcs; for example, were you to
sit and cross your legs at the knees and tap the crossing leg,
just below the kneecap, it would automatically jerk. You
couldn't stop this because the action is a reflex; what is
more, your leg could jerk that way all day without becoming
tired. Reflex action is not tiring. However, *prolonged tension
in muscles upsets tone* – the balance between relaxation and
contraction – *and also allows the chemicals of fatigue to
accumulate. So, aching begins.*

This is perhaps the main reason why nervously ill people so often complain of aching legs, aching back, aching neck and, less frequently, of aching arms.

The ache from tension is persistent, and should its victim have to stand, perhaps for only a few minutes, he will look around for support, preferably somewhere to sit, even lie, to relieve those heavy, aching, dragging legs. And yet there is nothing organically wrong with those legs: they are only fatigued through tension.

A feeling of weakness can also follow tension. Bend your right leg at the knee and fiercely tense it. Hold it that way for thirty seconds and then release it. Even after such a short spell of tension, it may feel shaky. The weakness of those shaky legs of nervous fatigue has such a simple explanation.

BLURRED VISION

Muscular fatigue can also affect the delicate muscles that accommodate the lens of the eye, so that vision may be blurred, especially on looking quickly from a near to a far object and vice versa. Also, objects in bright sunshine may appear as if in shadow. Although perhaps frightening, these upsets are temporary and unimportant; however, the sufferer with no knowledge of fatigue may think he is going blind and fear further attacks.

ALL-OVER HEADACHES

Tension in neck and scalp muscles can cause headache which may extend from above the eyes, over the top of the head, to the base of the skull and into the neck. There may also be very tender spots over the temples, at the base of the skull and down the sides of the trapezius – the stout muscle that helps support the head and anchor it to the body.

In addition, the head may feel so heavy, the scalp muscles so sore, that resting comfortably on the pillow at night may be difficult without a painkiller. For permanent cure, tension itself must be eased. However, knowing that tension is the cause of the pain (not brain tumour!) relieves some anxiety and hence some tension.

Much has been written today about removing tension, stress, by practising relaxing exercises. For nervously fatigued and nervously ill people, I recommend such exercise, at first directed by a competent teacher. If this is not practical I suggest discussion with their doctor.

We can be too anxious about always being relaxed and so may become tenser than usual. I advise relaxing at a set time, once or twice daily, and then worrying no more about it for the rest of the day. Such a daily routine can be built into our subconscious.

Relaxing through subconscious programming is more successful than becoming tense through constantly trying to remember to relax!

How we sit, stand and lie can be revealing. Trying to support the head in an uncomfortable position – for example, reading in bed or in a chair with an uncomfortable back – tenses head and neck muscles.

Having one's eyes on another job before finishing the one in hand is another guarantee of tension. A whirlwind can propel a toothbrush to finish its job when its owner spots dust on the shelf above the basin. Here again, the subconscious can be harnessed to help. Short, daily, routine practices at moving (cleaning teeth!) slowly will be enough to calm the whirlwind.

Although I mention treatment here, I reserve discussion of further treatment of the four nervous fatigues until later chapters.

4. Emotional fatigue

THE SECOND FATIGUE

If during stress our body always remained calm, we would feel no emotional fatigue and there would be many fewer sufferers of nervous illness. However, our body doesn't work that way. When nerves are subjected to stress, especially to strong emotions such as fear, for a long time, they can be aroused to record emotion with increasing intensity and often with unusual swiftness. They become trigger-happy and fire off at the slightest provocation. I call this aroused state *sensitisation*. Sensitisation of nerves is a most important part of nervous fatigue and consequently of nervous illness – of the anxiety state in particular to which, in my opinion, it is so often an important contributing cause.

When nerves are severely sensitised, emotion – especially fear – can seem to strike with physical force. The sufferer, rarely recognising this as sensitisation, becomes bewildered and afraid of it and so puts himself into a fear–adrenalin–fear cycle. This is the crucial point where so many people pass from being simply sensitised to becoming nervously ill.

To understand the fear–adrenalin–fear cycle we should understand how our nervous system works.

FEAR–ADRENALIN–FEAR CYCLE

Our nervous system consists of two divisions: voluntary and involuntary.

Voluntary nerves

By means of voluntary nerves we move our muscles more or less as we wish. The voluntary nervous system consists of the brain and spinal cord, from which a number of paired nerves arise, each ending in the muscle it supplies. The voluntary nerves are under our direct command – hence their name, voluntary.

Involuntary nerves

The involuntary nerves, with help from our glands, control the functioning of our organs: heart, lungs, bowels, etc., even the flow of saliva and sweat. The involuntary nervous system has its headquarters in a brain centre connected with a delicate network of fibres lying on either side of the spinal column (backbone) from which numerous thread-like branches pass to the internal organs.

Unlike the voluntary nerves they, with a few exceptions, are not under our direct control – hence their name, involuntary. However, they respond to, and register, our moods; for example, when afraid, our cheeks may blanch, our heart race, our blood pressure rise and our hands may sweat. We don't consciously do this and – what is so important in understanding nervous illness – we have no power to stop these reactions other than to change our mood.

The involuntary (sometimes called autonomic) nerves themselves consist of two divisions: sympathetic and parasympathetic. In a peaceful body these two hold each other in check. However, when under stress (for example, when we become angry, afraid, excited) one division dominates the other. In most people, under such circumstances, the sympathetic dominates the parasympathetic: the heart races, the blood pressure rises and so on. This is called the fight-or-flight response.

The action of the sympathetic nerves strengthens an animal's defences against the various dangers that beset it, such as extremes of temperature, deprivation of water, *attacks by its enemies.* Have you ever seen a frightened animal standing stock-still from fear before taking flight? Its nostrils and its pupils dilate, it breathes quickly. The sympathetic division of the involuntary nervous system has prepared it for fight or flight.

Sympathetic nerves are activated by hormones. A hormone, as defined by *Collins Australian Dictionary*, is a chemical substance formed in an endocrine gland and carried in the blood to another organ or tissue, where it has a specific effect. Several hormones are involved in sympathetic reaction to stress, but for the sake of simplicity I will speak only of adrenalin, the best known and perhaps the prime mover of all the hormones released by sympathetic nerves.

Occasionally, under stress, parasympathetic nerves dominate: pulse rate decreases, blood pressure falls. However, more usually the reaction is sympathetic, not parasympathetic, and when I speak of the fear–adrenalin–fear cycle I mean sympathetic reaction.

I will call the sympathetic nerves 'adrenalin-releasing nerves' here, because they are certainly not 'sympathetic', as we understand that word.

Among his many different symptoms, a sensitised person under stress, as well as feeling his heart beating unusually quickly, may feel it 'thump', 'miss' beats; he may have attacks of palpitation, feel his body vibrating with what he may describe as an electrical buzz; feel tremor, muscle jerks, muscle weakness, ringing in his limbs, churning stomach, light-headedness and so on, and above all, a spasm of fear may be felt as a flash of panic.

These symptoms can be so bewildering and upsetting that the sufferer may become more afraid of them than of the cause of his original stress.

Surely it can be understood how, by adding the extra stress of fear to his original stress, the sufferer stimulates the release of more and more adrenalin (and other stress hormones) and so further intensifies the symptoms he dreads, *which are themselves the symptoms of stress.*

This is the fear–adrenalin–fear cycle into which a sensitised person can easily be trapped and so placed on the way to nervous fatigue; perhaps nervous illness.

It is easy to add fear of fear when an original spasm of fear is felt as a scorching flash. Naturally the sufferer recoils from the flash and as he recoils, adds a second flash. I call these two fears first- and second-fear. Indeed, a sensitised person may be more concerned with his physical feeling of fear (usually panic) than with the original danger that brought it, and because that old bogey sensitisation prolongs the first flash, the two fears may feel like one. This is why a sufferer fails to recognise the two separate fears and so, fails to see how he prolongs his illness by adding the second fear. He resensitises himself with every spasm of second-fear. For him there is no greater enemy than his lack of understanding.

Fear-flashes 'I'm not quite sure what is making me afraid, but I have fear-flashes when I look at, or think, certain things; for example, I am afraid I may harm someone. Some days I may just have to look at someone, or touch something, to have that reaction. The picture may seem so clear, it blocks out everything else. This really frightens me.'

So many lives have been spoiled by a sensitised body's too acute reaction to some fearful thought. Without such exaggerated reaction, this woman could have reasoned with herself and been able to think, 'Of course I wouldn't harm anyone! How silly!' And that would be that. But when thoughts are accompanied by a strong stab of physical fear, the victim may be shocked and bewildered. At such a moment, it is natural to take the thoughts seriously and believe that perhaps he, or she, really could harm someone and so, perhaps, develop an obsession about it, as this woman has.

If only such people could understand that the thought frightens them only because of their body's sensitised reaction to it and not because it is a real threat. If only they could see the strength of their reaction as part of a physical (sensitised) state, unrelated to truth, and pass through the flash and continue on with the job on hand, how many lives could be saved from exhausting misery!

A nervously ill person may become so afraid of his symptoms that he may avoid places where he thinks stress will bring them on. Therefore, he may become afraid to leave the protection of his home. This condition is called agoraphobia. In my opinion, it is no more than *a particular stage* in an anxiety state.

It is important to understand that a person in an anxiety state (whether agoraphobic or not) may have continuous underlying sensitisation because he constantly resensitises himself with anxiety and fear.

SENSITISATION

SENSITISATION, IN A PERSON WITH NO FEAR OF IT, WOULD HEAL ITSELF.

As mentioned earlier, I stress the importance of sensitisation because it is the forerunner of emotional fatigue and therefore possibly also of nervous illness. The sequence is: stress (either sudden or gradual), then sensitisation, then bewilderment and fear. These are followed eventually by emotional fatigue and the added complications this brings – all possibly appearing finally as nervous illness.

Sensitisation is the prime cause of emotional fatigue, because, when severe, it exaggerates *all* emotions and so gradually depletes the sufferer's store of emotional energy. Having all emotions exaggerated is bewildering indeed and is one of the main reasons why a sensitised person sometimes thinks he must be going mad. For example, a slightly sad sight can seem tragic; a gloomy sight, overwhelmingly eerie; impatience can be felt as agitation; noise amplified until it seems intolerable; even a moment of joy can be felt hysterically. A sensitised person, feeling emotion as intensely as this, must inevitably become emotionally fatigued, feel 'drained'.

A nervously fatigued woman anxiously watched her old mother slump dejectedly as she walked up the garden path to a taxi waiting to take her to her one-roomed apartment and loneliness. Normally the daughter could have comforted herself with the thought that she would often visit her mother, would take her out, get her to join the Senior Citizens Club, perhaps get her interested in a hobby; but now in her sensitised anguish she could not convince herself of any of this. For her, there seemed only heartbreaking anxiety, and she wondered how long she could survive it.

Another nervously fatigued woman, while sight-seeing in England, visited some Roman Baths. These could seem a bit gruesome to anyone, but to her they were so eerie she could hardly restrain herself from running outside. She was bewildered by her strong reaction. I explained that sensitisation had exaggerated her feelings and that her agitated revulsion was only an intensified, sensitised version of the normal queasy feeling that anyone would get in the same situation.

Guilt

Most of us have some guilt tucked away that we have learned to live with without letting it upset us too much – but not so the sensitised person. Guilt shouts so loudly at home he feels he will never be reconciled to it. He sees no light at the end of that tunnel. Also, even if he struggles successfully with one guilt, sensitisation will soon present him with another. He has only to think of some guilt, perhaps up until now long forgotten, to immediately feel that frightening *whoosh*.

Some therapists say that a patient who comes with a list of guilty worries is 'that kind of person' – always looking for something to worry or feel guilty about. He may be, but more likely he is sensitised. Unfortunately, instead of an explanation of sensitisation, medication is too often the only remedy prescribed.

Also, some therapists make too much of guilt simply because the patient does; so while the sufferer may take only one or two small guilts to his therapist, he may leave with a heavy bundle.

The impulse to confess guilt is strong while emotional and fatigued; the urge to be relieved of that heavy load on the chest is so insistent. However, a sufferer should beware of yielding to such an urge while sensitised. Confessing guilt can sometimes complicate, not comfort. How essential it is to understand sensitisation. (I discuss coping with guilt in Chapter 22.)

Thunder in the street

Sensitisation can also exaggerate noise. Heavy vehicles can sound like thunder in the street and sitting through a noisy movie can feel like torture. The person, who does not understand that noise is temporarily amplified by sensitised auditory nerves, is naturally bewildered and this is increased by the strength of the force that grips and incites him to 'rush away from it all'.

Love intensified

More bewildering still (as if he hasn't had enough already!), even pleasant experiences can be exaggerated; for example, the intensity of the love felt at no more than the sight of a loved one's hand can move the sensitised person to tears.

Joy felt hysterically

And, as already mentioned, a rare moment of joy can be felt hysterically. A nervously ill man described how, on one occasion when standing beside a piano while a friend played the accompaniment to a rollicking song, he joined in the singing.

When they finished, his friend turned and said, 'Don't tell me you're depressed and ill! You sang that better than any of us. You seemed deliriously happy!' The man explained to me, 'Doctor, if they only knew! While I was singing I felt more manic than happy. In fact, delirious was the right word. That was how I felt. If only I could stay just a little bit happy and not the way I am – way up one minute and down the next. They haven't a clue, doctor!'

The shock of waking

Also a sensitised body can react to the slightest shock. Even the mild shock of waking from sleep can make a heart race. This may be accompanied by such a strong feeling of foreboding the sufferer may need to keep reassuring himself that nothing terrible has happened, or is about to happen.

Such a person, fearing anxiety so intensely, may become so susceptible to it that the mere hint of its approach can grip 'the pit of his stomach' with a gnawing ache – and how he longs for a comforting word to ease that ache. Sensitisation can be a real stomach-gripper!

Also, while he is so responsive to anxious thought, the slightest hazard his imagination may conjure up seems overwhelming; for example, if he tosses at night and cannot sleep, the sensitised person easily imagines he will never be able to sleep properly again. And what a response he gets from his sensitised body!

Because of such a flashing response to any anxious thought, he may feel powerless to make decisions, be embarrassingly suggestible and so become gradually bereft of confidence. At this stage he may feel as if his personality has disintegrated, as if both he and the world are unreal.

Waking early: the morning's knife edge The upsetting symptoms that can come to a nervous person on waking have been called the startle syndrome. Sensitised nerves can be startled by the slight shock of waking even though the waker may not recognise any shock. Also the sufferer may go to bed at night feeling relieved and peaceful, only to wake the next morning and feel the same old familiar feeling of foreboding. The optimistic feelings of the night before seem to have little influence on the mood of the next morning. The feeling of foreboding may seem so real that the sufferer may search for some impending trouble to explain it. Also, when he first wakes, his nerves may be so 'raw' he feels as if he is balanced on a knife's edge. This is a legacy from the tension of the previous days. Even when the sufferer is almost recovered, some slight renewed stress may bring on again a few mornings of startle and foreboding. Why worry!

Getting up, going to the bathroom, making a hot drink may be enough to break the spell. At least the sufferer should let the feelings come; not try to push them away. He should relax toward them.

We describe some people with exaggerated reactions (not necessarily nervously fatigued or nervously ill) as unbalanced, and a sensitised person certainly feels this way. He may feel this imbalance so acutely that he begins to think he is some sort of weakling. One man said desperately, 'I am the exact opposite to what I used to be, to what I really am. What is happening?' He did not understand that this feeling of imbalance was temporary and was no more than his body's sensitised expression of ordinary, normal emotion. Small wonder that one so buffeted by emotion is incredulous when told that his suffering is no more than sensitised nerves exaggerating normal reaction and that when freed from the effects of tension, sensitisation can heal itself. This is why understanding sensitisation and the part it plays in causing emotional fatigue is so important: UNDERSTANDING IN ITSELF RELEASES SOME TENSION.

The exhaustion following prolonged, exaggerated emotional reaction (especially if accompanied by upsetting physical nervous symptoms: quickly beating heart, 'missed' heartbeats, churning stomach and so on) is especially bewildering because (1) it can seem incapacitatingly severe and yet be so little related to physical effort and so little relieved by resting and (2) is so difficult to describe and so rarely understood by those who have never felt it, including the family and even the doctor.

One nervously ill woman said, 'I feel as if my whole body is a "nothing", doctor! I haven't the strength to pull it together and yet my husband keeps saying, "For God's sake, pull yourself together, Jess! How can you be so tired, when you've done nothing all day!"'

We can survive long periods of stress providing that our glands – principally pituitary and adrenal – can continue to supply essential hormones. The body adapts to stress. However, if adaptation fails (glands become depleted) we pass to the stage of exhaustion. This is why emotional exhaustion – based on glandular depletion – is not appreciably related to physical effort nor appreciably helped by rest, but is almost miraculously helped by release from emotional suffering and so from stress.

Apathy and depression warn of approaching depletion. First comes apathy. As I say later in this book, even to comb his hair can become such an effort that the sufferer begins to look unkempt and no longer cares.

With further depletion, apathy becomes depression. The depression of nervous illness is almost invariably caused by emotional depletion.

The symptoms and experiences I have been describing may sound frightening. However, they are less frightening when one understands the simple patterns of their development and that recovery lies in reversing that pattern, as I show later. There is no particular bogey; no compelling outside force. There is only a body's natural reaction to stress – and the body will react just as naturally by healing itself when stress is removed. And much stress is removed simply by understanding.

5. Mental fatigue

THE THIRD FATIGUE

The sensitised, fatigued person is naturally concerned about himself, 'how he feels', so his anxious thoughts often (sometimes constantly) turn inward. Much anxious introspection brings mental fatigue, just as concentrated study can bring brain-fatigue in a student. Arthur Rubinstein, speaking at the Juilliard School of Music, advised pupils to practise no more than three or four hours a day; any longer, he said, was wasted time because the mind could not absorb it.

When the mind is fresh, thoughts can flit lightly from subject to subject. In a severely mentally fatigued person, thoughts come haltingly and sometimes so slowly that thinking is an effort, almost as if each thought has to be selected and placed individually in the sentence. Speech may therefore be hesitant, even sometimes stuttering.

The sufferer may also become confused and find concentrating and remembering difficult. Forgetting immediate events can be so persistent the sufferer may suspect he is going prematurely senile.

Talking can be such a strain for a mentally tired person that if he sees a neighbour approaching he will cross the street rather than talk to him. He may sometimes begin a sentence and feel too tired to finish it.

Before he was so mentally tired, he could spend hours on the weekend sitting in the sun, lazily dipping into the newspapers, scarcely thinking at all as time slipped by, but now he watches time consciously, almost every second of it. And how those seconds drag; an hour can seem like eternity to a mentally fatigued person.

Normally we rest our mind during the moments when we look and listen without concentrating too intensely; unimportant thoughts flit so lightly from subject to subject we are hardly aware of them: the funny design on the new ironing-board cover, the shine of the leaves of the copper beech tree. However, when mentally fatigued thoughts do not flit, they seem to stick. This is one reason why a mentally tired person gnaws at a worry, feeling unable to release it, especially if the worry holds fear.

When thoughts 'stick' and are accompanied by fear, the way is prepared for the development of obsessions, phobias. So many obsessions and phobias *begin in this simple way*.

An obsession is a thought that preoccupies a mind to an abnormal degree and this is exactly what can happen to a sensitised person suffering from mental fatigue, when a repeated 'sticky' thought that frightens comes with such force that it seems to propel its victim almost physically. Surely it is understandable how obsession can be born at this point? Understanding this is extremely important because with understanding, obsession loses its mystery and so, some of its power to frighten.

A fairly common obsession is doubt about loving one's spouse. A nervously ill woman said that although she knew she really loved her husband, the thought that she didn't kept recurring so frequently and with such force, she was beginning to think it was true. Of course it was her sensitised response to this fear and its repetition in her tired mind that was convincing her. When sensitisation and mental fatigue come together, throwing off frightening thoughts can seem impossible.

This woman found that the inability to disregard her upsetting thoughts, although in her heart she knew them to be false, was one more proof that she was going mad. How many nervously fatigued, or nervously ill, people have thought this! And of course, the more frightened she felt, the more sensitised she became and the more overpowering and persistent were her thoughts.

She admitted that the thought about not loving her husband was most convincing and stuck most tenaciously when she was tired. She also said there were moments when she could see this thought for what it really was: no more than a silly thought in a very tired mind. At such times the idea seemed so absurd, she could smile at it. I call these flashes of normal thinking, glimpsing. I discuss curing obsession by glimpsing in a later chapter.

A phobia is an irrational, persistent fear. This can develop very simply in a sensitised person. While mental fatigue makes the development more likely, sensitisation alone can be enough. A sensitised person, while waiting in a queue, instead of feeling normal exasperation, can feel agitated panic and from then on may avoid standing in any queue, so developing a queue phobia. In this simple way many phobias arise. Understandably simple, isn't it?

'MUZZY' HEAD

A mentally fatigued person may say his mind feels enveloped in a blanket, feels dull, heavy, thick. This may be aggravated by blurred vision and perhaps a tendency to stagger slightly (accompanying muscular fatigue). Some say they feel as if a good hard crack on the head would clear it.

In mental fatigue an attack of muzzy head may last from a few hours, to days. As one woman described it, 'I seem to have a wall in my head that my thoughts knock against. It's very hard to concentrate; before, I always had a very clear head and good insight. But this muzzy head! When it clears I can think very well, but when it descends, I'm finished!

'I had a guilty experience about which I worried so much, I couldn't get this worry off my mind. My psychiatrist told me that I was punishing myself and put me on medication. This helped, but this "thing" came back again. I would have a clear head for half an hour and in that time I could talk, even laugh, and then all of a sudden, I would remember the guilt, start crying inwardly and the muzzy head would descend.'

Not recognising her muzziness as a combination of brain-fatigue and tension, she became alarmed by it, so added to her problem stress, more tension, more brooding and therefore, more brain-fatigue.

While imprisoned by this blanket of mental fatigue, a sufferer, because of slowed thinking and muzzy head, may become aware of a pressing consciousness of self – especially of his actions, his thoughts. This inward-thinking, as I call it, may persist after most of the other symptoms of nervous illness have gone; indeed, it is sometimes the last symptom with which he has to contend.

He rarely recognises it as that old bogey, mental fatigue, still at work, binding his mind in the tracks it has been following for the previous months or years.

Exasperation at being caught in this trap brings more inward-thinking, more stress, more tension – a frightening cycle – and the harder he tries to escape from it, the more bound within it he feels.

This cycle of fatigue and sensitisation working together is following simple, natural laws that can be reversed. Inward-thinking can be cured, as I show later.

Out of the bog Many people trying to recover from nervous illness have the feeling that they must struggle up, up, out of some depth, almost as if they have to drag themselves out of some kind of bog to finally feel on top of things; on the same level as life around them. For example, when they hear of a friend going on holiday they think of him as being 'on the same level!' as the place he is going to – he has only to pack a case and be off! Whereas, for the sufferer, going for a holiday would seem like going to somewhere in the sky above: far, far out of reach.

He does not understand that he feels like this because, to face travelling, he would have to come 'out of himself', 'up from the depths'; up, out of his grey world of introspection. And it is a grey world. The sun may shine, but his mind is so dulled by tiring, endless, anxious introspection, his eye muscles so tensed by anxiety, that the world may actually look grey.

Also, to simply be on the same daily level as other people (with no thought of a holiday) seems to require energy he thinks he will never have. The bog is so deep and clinging!

Time, more time and acceptance make the impossible gradually possible. The bog becomes dry land.

SUDDEN GLARE SHOCKS!

A mentally fatigued person, especially when used to the shade and shelter of indoors, can feel sudden shock on opening the front door and facing the light. Later in this book, I describe a mentally fatigued, nervously ill man who is obliged to pass through a dark tunnel before emerging onto a sunlit beach packed with people and gay umbrellas. He is so shocked by the sudden brightness, he feels unreal, like a sleep-walker. The shock arrests his thoughts and gives him insight into the greyness of the world he has been living in – a world of constant anxious introspection – and he recognises this greyness as no more than persistent mental fatigue.

The experience helps him recover. For the first time he understands the meaning of mental fatigue, and becomes aware of how absorbingly bound he has been in his own anxious thoughts. He can see now that his trouble was not so much the gravity of his problems as the fatigued state he was in. This comes as a revelation because for weeks he had been desperately gnawing at those problems thinking that they were insoluble. Understanding helped release him.

6. Fatigue of the spirit

THE FOURTH FATIGUE

Finally, there is fatigue of the spirit. When a nervously fatigued person is so depleted that every action, perhaps every thought, is an effort, he begins to wonder if the struggle is worth it. Some say they feel as if they have been suddenly precipitated into old age; that they haven't the strength to face another day, let alone weeks, months. The will to survive falters, especially if the sufferer has been trying to recover by fighting his way out of fatigue. The best way to increase fatigue is to try to fight it, as I will show in later chapters.

First, the fatigued spirit must somehow find fresh hope and courage. The merest glimmer is enough to begin with. It may have to be, because even that can seem too much for an exhausted spirit to resurrect. However, recovery can build on such a slender foundation, so slender, that at the slightest puff of discouragement, it may seem to collapse.

And yet, if there is understanding and a plan for recovery instead of a hopeless no-man's land, hope and courage do grow again, as bravely as the green shoots grow on the burnt-out tree-stumps in a forest ravaged by fire.

I have seen so many people take those first shaky steps to recovery holding desperately on to such slender hope and courage, sustained by the understanding I have been privileged to give them.

Although those first steps may seem weak and faltering, they hold the same indomitable strength that has carried us all through millions of years of our evolutionary struggle.

We all have this strength, this power, within us, and it will work miracles if we trust it to help us learn to walk and live with fear, so that we can eventually walk and live without fear.

Old age or nervous illness? 'How does one cope with getting old and at the same time, with the remnants of nervous illness? My illness seems to be taken over by the feelings of advancing age. I'm making no real progress that I can see because of not being able to cope with work or pleasure, or even with a journey by car to go on holiday. And yet I've lived through fifteen years of nervous illness! This feeling of great effort takes me back years to the days when I was first going downhill. Perhaps this is why I feel that the cause is now not so much illness as old age.

'The things about the house and garden that I used to do, even when I felt bad, I can't get the strength to do now. If I make myself do them I get tired with aches and pains and it doesn't seem worthwhile. I'm sure there's a link between feeling this way now and the years spent in nervous illness while life was hell. I'm sure I'm feeling the result of this more now because I'm older.'

Your tiredness is probably more a legacy of illness than of age, although you don't say how old you are – you talk only of 'advancing' years. Naturally resilience and energy decrease with age and with them go motivation and, so often, interest. Usually the change is gradual, whereas I suspect that you feel old suddenly.

Prolonged nervous illness brings fatigue of the spirit and, in my opinion, this is probably your main trouble. While you were struggling to recover earlier, it was not so much that you were younger as that you had a goal and hope – two prime motivators. Now you are not only tired by the struggle, you have also lost confidence because you know you are growing old and therefore think that feeling tired is irrevocable.

If you have the courage to replace despair with fresh hope and willingness to accept once more, you will gradually feel strength return. Peace of mind is a wonderful healer and you apparently have little of that now.

Your question has been asked of me many times. I have found that if the questioner stops trying to fathom how much fatigue is the result of nervous illness and how much of old age, and instead does what he can within the limits of his present strength without thrashing himself too severely with doubt and bewilderment, he is surprised how much he can gradually do. Our bodies have great recuperative powers if we remove tension – even in our eighties. I have proved this on myself.

Also, many nervously ill people do not lead active lives during their illness and suffer from lack of exercise – muscles become flabby and legs tire so easily that sitting or lying, instead of walking, is a constant temptation.

Even the memory of tiredness can bring a feeling of fatigue, and as for the thought of facing 'it all' again . . . ! Small wonder you baulk at it.

My advice is: don't look for progress; take each day as it comes, doing what must be done without asking too many questions. Don't protest too vehemently; that wastes strength.

Be sure you eat enough nourishing food and are not taking medication habitually or a too heavy dose of sleeping pills at night. As we grow older we tolerate drugs poorly; small doses can have big effects. Also, if you are only picking at food, I suggest a moderate dose of vitamins.

Once more, acceptance; but with a fresh heart.

7. Nervous fatigue and nervous illness

It may be difficult for a sufferer from nervous fatigue to appreciate the difference between his fatigue and nervous illness. Some – particularly executives struggling to hold down an important and stressful job, indeed anyone trying to do a day's work that seems beyond their ability to cope – may suspect that, if not already suffering from nervous illness, they are at least threatened by it. So they have two struggles, one with their fatigue and another with their fear of it becoming illness. This struggle is particularly poignant because in their exhausted state their fear of nervous illness can open the door to it.

Understanding his symptoms and experiences will at least relieve the nervously fatigued person of bewilderment. Also, with understanding he is less likely to become afraid of 'the state he is in' and although perhaps tottering with fatigue, can keep himself free from actual nervous illness.

However, if fear, through ignorance, takes control, the fatigued person often flounders in despair, almost blindly reaching for help. At this time the right guidance is crucial. Many years of experience in helping hundreds of nervously fatigued and nervously ill people have proved that the guidance I now offer, if followed, will bring peace.

It becomes confusing to talk about nervously fatigued and nervously ill people and at the same time try to differentiate between them. So, henceforth, I will speak to the nervously ill, although stressing that much of the advice given applies equally to the nervously fatigued.

8. What is nervous illness?

You will appreciate that there are different grades of 'nervous' suffering. Countless people have 'bad nerves' and many of them, although distressed, continue at their work and cannot be said to suffer from nervous breakdown. Indeed, while they readily admit to having 'bad nerves', they would indignantly refute any suggestion of breakdown. And yet a nervous breakdown is no more than an intensification of their symptoms. Although this book is concerned mainly with the development and treatment of nervous breakdown, almost every symptom complained of by people with 'bad nerves' will be found here, and such people will recognise themselves again and again in the patients with breakdown described in the following chapters. The symptoms are the same, it is but their severity that varies. The person with breakdown feels these symptoms so much more intensely.

Where do 'bad nerves' end and where does nervous breakdown begin? By nervous breakdown we mean a state in which a person's 'nervous' symptoms are so intense that they cope inadequately with their daily work or do not cope at all. Doctors are asked if people really 'break', and if so,

how? We are also asked how a nervous breakdown begins
and develops.

THE BREAKING POINT

Many people are tricked into breakdown. A sudden or
prolonged state of stress may sensitise adrenalin-releasing
nerves to produce the symptoms of stress in an exaggerated,
alarming way. This state of sensitisation is well known to
doctors, but so little known to people generally that, when
first experienced, it may bewilder and then dupe its victim
into becoming afraid of it. If asked to pinpoint the beginning
of nervous breakdown, I would say that it is at the moment
when sensitised people become afraid of the sensations
produced by severe stress and so place themselves in a cycle
of fear–adrenalin–fear. In response to this fear, more
adrenalin is released and the already sensitised body is thus
stimulated to produce even more and more intense
sensations, which inspire more fear. This is the
fear–adrenalin–fear cycle.

TWO TYPES OF BREAKDOWN

Most breakdowns are of two main types. One is relatively
straightforward and its victim is mainly concerned with
the distressing sensations brought by sensitised nerves. In
such people, nerves may be suddenly sensitised by the
stress of some shock, such as an exhausting surgical
operation, a severe haemorrhage, an accident, a difficult
pregnancy or labour; or, sensitisation may come more
gradually following a debilitating illness, anaemia, or too

strenuous dieting. This person is often happy in their domestic life and work; indeed, they may have no great problem other than the inability, because of breakdown, to cope with normal responsibilities.

The second type of breakdown is begun by some overwhelming problem, conflict, sorrow, guilt or disgrace. The stress of prolonged, fearful introspection gradually sensitises nerves to react more and more intensely to the anxious introspection, until bewilderment and fear of the strange feelings sensitisation brings, even of the strange thoughts it may bring, become as much part of the suffering as the original problem, conflict, sorrow, guilt or disgrace. Indeed, it may eventually be the main concern.

9. The simpler forms of nervous illness

People suffering from the first type of breakdown (anxiety neurosis), complain of some, or all, of the following symptoms of sensitised involuntary nerves: sleeplessness, depression, fatigue, churning stomach, indigestion, racing heart, banging heart, shaking heart, palpitations, 'missed' heartbeats, a sharp knife-like pain under the heart, a sore feeling around the heart, sweating hands, 'pins and needles' in the hands and feet, a choking feeling in the throat, an inability to take a deep breath, a tight feeling across the chest, 'ants' or 'worms' crawling under the skin, a tight band of pain around the head, giddiness, and strange tricks of vision such as the apparent movement of inanimate objects. Nausea, vomiting, occasional diarrhoea, and frequent desire to pass urine may be added to the picture.

The following is a typical list brought to the doctor by such a patient. This was brought by a young mother. It is printed exactly as she wrote it:

- All tied up
- Headaches
- Tired and weary
- Palpitations
- Dreadful
- Nervous
- Sharp pain under the heart
- No interest
- Restless
- My heart beats like lead
- I have a heavy lump of dough in my stomach
- Heart-shakes

Sufferers from these symptoms are easily upset by little things. They are quite certain that there is something seriously wrong with them and cannot believe that anyone else could have had such a distressing experience. Many feel convinced that they have a brain tumour (at least something 'deep-seated') or that they are on the verge of madness. Their one wish is to be, as quickly as possible, the person they used to be before this 'horrible thing' happened to them. They are often not aware that their symptoms are nervous in origin and follow a well-recognised pattern shared by numerous sufferers like themselves, *the pattern of continuous fear and tension.*

I shall describe in detail the development of such a breakdown before discussing cure, because bewilderment at what is happening and fear of what may happen next are often the main factors prolonging illness.

THE BEGINNING: PALPITATIONS

Many healthy people are precipitated into this type of nervous breakdown by the fear induced by some sudden, alarming, yet harmless bodily sensation such as their first unexpected attack of palpitations. Even a healthy heart may palpitate when anaemic, fatigued or under stress. Such an attack can be frightening to a highly strung temperament, especially if it comes at night and there is no one to turn to for comfort and reassurance. The heart races wildly and the sufferer is sure it will burst. They usually lie still, afraid to move for fear of further damage. So fear arises. It is only natural to be alarmed by sudden, unexpected, uncomfortable happenings in our body, particularly in the region of our heart.

As described earlier, under 'Fear–adrenalin–fear cycle', fear causes an additional outpouring of adrenalin, so that a heart already stirred to palpitations becomes further excited, beats even more quickly and the attack lasts longer. The sufferer may panic, thinking they are about to die. Hands sweat, the face burns, fingers tingle with 'pins and needles', while they wait for they know not what.

The attack eventually stops – it always does – and all may be well for a while. However, having had one frightening experience, he dreads another and for days remains tense and anxious, from time to time feeling his pulse. If the palpitations do not return he settles down, loses himself in his work and forgets the incident. If, however, he has a second attack, he really is concerned. Apparently the wretched thing has come to stay!

Not only is he afraid of palpitating, but he is also in a state of tension wondering what further alarming experience his body may have in store for him. It is not long before tension, releasing more and more adrenalin, makes his stomach churn, his hands sweat and his heart constantly beat quickly. He becomes even more afraid, and still more adrenalin is released. In other words, he becomes caught in the fear–adrenalin–fear cycle.

TENSION THROUGH FEAR

At this stage the sufferer consults a doctor, who usually succeeds in reassuring him and banishing his fear. However, he may not be sufficiently reassured and may be unfortunate enough to be put to bed and advised to 'take things carefully' and to 'be sure not to overdo it'. When so advised the average person, particularly if young and not yet protected by the philosophy of age, lies in bed brooding over his 'bad' heart, afraid to move for fear of straining it further. This patient was already in a state of nervous tension worrying about the palpitations. Can you imagine his tension now? Perhaps you have experienced it?

On the other hand, should the doctor, in an effort to reassure, make too light of the palpitations, the patient may stay in bed of his own volition, convinced that the doctor is withholding the worst and has not told him all. If he remains tensed and afraid he is certain to have further attacks, and the more frequently they come the more he hugs the couch. The more he rests, the more time he has to brood and the more tense and apprehensive he becomes. His finger is continually hovering above his pulse, and in response to this anxiety his heart constantly beats quicker than it should, although not as fast as when palpitating. Actually he thinks it is beating faster than it is, because he is conscious of every beat. To him it is thumping, banging, racing. One ingenious man arranged his pillows end to end, so that he could lay his ear on the crack between them – in this way he thought he heard less thumping.

The sufferer by now is really sorry for himself. He loses appetite, loses weight and dreads being alone 'for fear of having a turn'; at the same time he is afraid to be with people for fear of having one and making a fool of himself. It is not long before he develops most of the sensations of breakdown – the churning stomach, sweating hands, pains around the heart, racing heart, giddy turns, headache – in other words, the full fear–adrenalin–fear cycle.

If fear of palpitations has not drawn this person into this type of nervous breakdown, fear of some other upsetting bodily sensation generally has. Perhaps he has had pain in the region of his heart which he, in alarm and ignorance, diagnoses as angina. Perhaps a strenuous, anxious, highly tensed life has given him a constantly churning stomach or 'shaking' heart at which he becomes alarmed. Whatever the cause, in answer to his continuous apprehension his adrenalin-releasing nerves become sensitised and gradually burden his day with the new, upsetting sensations described above. He tries to fight or escape, until he too becomes caught in the same fear–adrenalin–fear cycle as the person afraid of the palpitations.

As mentioned, these people have these sensations as a more or less constant background to their day. They may have moments of respite; for example, some on waking feel strangely calm and may be able to lie at peace for an hour or so before the churning starts. Others feel calmest at night. Others know no peace.

PANIC

Some people, as well as having this background of disturbing sensations, are swept from time to time by intense waves of panic. Some have a panic spasm every few minutes, and this may continue for hours. It will be appreciated how disturbing these spasms can be when the sufferer is working and trying to appear normal and how they live in dread of the spasms coming at inappropriate moments. Unfortunately they are most likely to come at such times, as the person is then most apprehensive and afraid.

It is possible that the recurring attacks of palpitation have now left the sufferer, who is more concerned with the other manifestations of fear, although it is more usual to find the palpitations continuing and adding to the miserable burden.

This is not a far-fetched story. I have heard it so often that I give it respectful attention. I have known this stage, inadequately treated, to last several years, the patient going from doctor to doctor.

To healthy people this history may sound all too childish and stupid. They think, 'Why doesn't he pull up his socks and get on with his work and forget all this nonsense?' That is exactly what he would like to do. But what we, the healthy ones, do not realise is that by this time the fear felt by such a sufferer is greater than any the average person has known or has paused to imagine. Repeated spasms of panic, when accompanied by exhaustion, not only increase in intensity but need less and less to start them. Dread of having them may bring on a whole sequence. Meeting a stranger, the thought of being left alone, even a slamming door may suffice. Also, in spite of a great desire to pull up his socks and get to work, such frequent, intense spasms of fear seem to paralyse his will to act.

Some years ago, when recuperating from an operation, I stayed with friends who were planning a bush walk. They asked a young man to join us. It was not a long walk, they assured me (but long enough for me, thought I, as I looked at his long legs). To my astonishment this big fellow soon fell behind and we frequently had to wait for him to catch up. At lunch he lay exhausted on the grass. Later he told me his story. For years, since student days, he had had recurring spasms of intense panic, so that his life had become a nightmare. He was not afraid of anything in particular, only the feeling of fear itself, and this had become so intensified and exhausting that even that short walk had been too much.

This man was eventually cured and able to lead a scientific expedition. I mention him because he was no weakling but a clever scientist in a responsible position. With help he recovered quickly, after having suffered for ten years.

FIGHTING

The sufferer from nervous breakdown is neither fool nor coward, but often a remarkably brave person who fights his breakdown to the best of his ability with commendable although often misdirected courage. He may fight through almost every waking moment, with sweating hands and tensed muscles, agitatedly trying to force forgetfulness of his desperate state by consciously concentrating on other things. Or he may pace the floor of his mind, anxiously searching for a way out of his miserable prison, only to meet one closed door after another.

At night he falls into bed exhausted, to sleep the fretful sleep of nervous agitation, the heavy sleep of nervous exhaustion, the drugged sleep of the barbiturate swallower, or, worse still, to find no sleep in spite of heavy sedation.

At times the early part of the evening may not seem so bad. He may feel almost normal and think he has conquered this 'thing' at last, and may go to bed saying, 'Now, that's the finish. Tomorrow I will be my old self again,' only to wake and find the spasms and the churning worse than ever. He cannot understand why, having felt so much better by evening, he should wake the next morning feeling as ill as ever, perhaps even worse. He certainly feels more hopeless, if that be possible. He is either convinced that there is some short, quick road to recovery which continually eludes him, or that there is not, and never could be, a way back to peace from such suffering as his.

He looks back with longing at the person he used to be, the person who could sit peacefully and enjoy a good book, or happily watch television, and he apprehensively counts the weeks, months, even years, since he was that person. He reasons that if he cannot become himself again by fighting, how else can he? Fighting is his natural defence, the only weapon he knows, so he fights even harder. But the harder he fights, the worse he becomes. Naturally – for fighting means more tension, tension more adrenalin and further stimulation of the adrenalin-releasing nerves, and so the continuation of symptoms. To make matters worse, his friends do not hesitate to advise him to fight it. Even his doctor may say, 'You'll have to fight this thing. You mustn't let it get the better of you!'

What has happened to him he cannot understand. He is like a person possessed. He does not realise that there is no devil sitting on his shoulder and that he is simply doing this to himself with fear, fight, and flight from fear.

It is at this stage that he may develop severe headache which he likens to an iron band encircling his head, or to a weight pressing on top of it. He may be giddy, nauseated, have difficulty in expanding his chest to take in a deep breath, feel a heavy soreness around his heart or a sharp pain under it which he sometimes refers to as 'the dagger'. He may also have recurring 'funny turns' such as spells of abnormally slowly beating heart, 'missed' heartbeats and weak, trembling turns. He loses interest in everything and in everybody, and mounting tension makes him easily upset by trifles.

COLLAPSE

Finally the day may come when, yielding to some extra burden of fear, the sufferer gives up what she thinks is her last ounce of strength, and 'collapses', while the alarmed family stand round helplessly. The words heard murmured in the hall, 'Doctor, she has collapsed,' close a chapter for her and act as chains to bind her to the bed. If she could not find her way out of breakdown while on her two feet she wonders how she will find it now that she has collapsed. The fight seems too great, the journey too uphill, so she may spend weeks, even months, on her back, or be taken promptly to hospital for intensive treatment.

THE CONSTANT PATTERN OF FEAR

No doubt you have recognised some of yourself in these people and it may be a revelation to find that the basis of your mysterious symptoms is, like theirs, fear.

Whether breakdown be mild or severe, the basic cause is fear. Conflict, sorrow, guilt or disgrace may start a breakdown, but it is not long before fear takes command. Even great sorrow at the loss of a loved one is mixed with fear, the fear of facing the future alone. Sexual problems are most likely to cause breakdown when accompanied by fear or guilt. Guilt opens the door to fear. Anxiety, worry and dread are only variants of fear in different guises.

It could be argued that strain, as distinct from fear, may cause breakdown in certain situations. For example, there is much prolonged strain for a middle-aged woman tending an old, sick parent. However, while she copes from day to day, does not look too far ahead and does not think it too important that she is chained to her duties, she can sustain months, years, of such strain. She may 'bend' and need help from time to time, but she will not 'break'.

I once commented on the ability of one woman to carry on for so long in such a situation and was told by her brother, 'Yes, it is a great strain on Nadia, but she never did think of herself.' That was the key to Nadia's endurance. Had she listened to her sympathising friends, begun to feel sorry for herself and come to dread the future, she would have sown the seeds of a nervous breakdown.

Strain may cause severe headaches (Nadia had migraine) and physical exhaustion, but unless accompanied by fear it will not cause the incapacity known as nervous breakdown. When work threatens to become beyond our physical strength and our responsibilities demand that we keep going, fear usually comes into the picture and any ensuing breakdown is caused not by the exhaustion, as so many believe, but by the fears it brings.

AFRAID TO ADMIT FEAR

Sometimes it is difficult to admit even to yourself that you are afraid. One woman insisted that it was the 'stomach-shakes', not fear, that caused her nervousness. So I avoided the word 'fear' when talking to her and tried to convince her that it was 'tension' causing her stomach-shakes. Her stomach had 'shaken' for six months; she had eaten and slept little and looked the wreck she felt, and yet when she finally accepted that the shakes depended on the excretion of adrenalin through tension, she was able to relax and lose them within a month. However, she continued to insist that she had not been afraid of them.

Is it possible to explain the disappearance of this woman's symptoms in any other way than that she had lost her fear of them? I asked her for an explanation and she said, 'I disliked them. I lost my dislike of them.' She had disliked them so much that she had let them dominate her life for six months. Surely the difference between such strong dislike and fear is only one of degree? At least we have to admit that strong dislike of physical sensations is so close to fear that it can cause the same nervous reactions.

Camouflage your fear as intense dislike if it makes you feel happier. This is of no importance, as long as you understand that the physical reactions in your body to intense dislike and fear are so similar that any difference is negligible.

That persistent inner voice There is a persistent inner voice that challenges the nervous person to think the worst; a little voice that says, 'Others can do it, others can recover, but not you!' A nervously ill person's mind can play strange tricks and he is too easily impressed by them. He doesn't understand that it is natural for an inner voice to complain as his does, while he is still so sensitised.

Recovery often follows similar patterns and one of these is the frequent development of a negative inner voice. Obstructive thoughts are normal, very human, in the circumstances. Their voice should be heard; let it have its way, it will take it, anyhow. Let it say what it wants to; let it bring plenty of fear but *watch it doing*

it; while you have the courage to watch without letting
it overpower you, you will gradually feel yourself
becoming detached from its babbling.

THE SINGLE PATTERN

The breakdown described in this chapter was not
complicated by a particular problem. It was caused by no
more than fear of the very feelings that fear itself had
aroused, and as such is the commonest and most
straightforward form of breakdown we know. If yours is this
type of breakdown, it is a step toward cure to see your
various symptoms as part of a single pattern coming from a
single cause, fear. These symptoms are not peculiar to you,
but are well known to many like you. And yet, however
distressing they may be, I assure you that every unwelcome
sensation can be banished and you can regain peace of mind
and body.

10. How to cure the simpler form of nervous illness

If you have this type of breakdown you will notice that, as already mentioned, you have certain symptoms as a fairly constant background to your day, while others come from time to time. For example, the churning stomach, sweating hands and rapidly beating heart are more or less always with you, while fear-spasms, palpitations, 'missed' heartbeats, pains around the heart, trembling turns, breathlessness, giddiness and vomiting come in attacks, at intervals. The constant symptoms are those of sustained fear, hence their chronicity (being chronic), while the different recurring attacks are the result of varying intensity in sustained fear, hence their periodicity (occurring periodically).

The treatment of all symptoms depends on a few simple rules. When you first read them you may think, 'This is too simple for me. It will take something more drastic to cure me.' In spite of this, you will need to be shown how to apply this simple treatment and may often have to re-read instructions.

The principle of treatment can be summarised as:

- facing
- accepting
- floating
- letting time pass

There is nothing mysterious or surprising about this treatment, and yet it is enlightening to see how many people sink deeper into their breakdown by doing the exact opposite.

Let us look again briefly at the people described in the last chapter, afraid of the physical feelings aroused by fear, and see if we can pinpoint their own treatment of their breakdown.

First, the man became unduly alarmed by his symptoms, examining each as it appeared, 'listening in' in apprehension. He tried to free himself of the unwelcome feelings by tensing himself to meet them or by pushing them away, agitatedly seeking occupation to force forgetfulness. In other words, by fighting or running away.

Also, he was bewildered because he could not find a cure overnight. He kept looking back and worrying because so much time was passing and he was not yet cured, as if this thing were an evil spirit which could be exorcised if only he, or the doctor, knew the trick. *He was impatient with time.*

Briefly, he spent his time:

- running away, not facing
- fighting, not accepting
- arresting and 'listening in', not floating past
- being impatient with time, not letting time pass

Now, let us consider how you can cure yourself by *facing*, *accepting*, *floating* and *letting time pass*.

11. Facing

Facing means acknowledging that cure must come from inside you – with guidance and help from outside, of course – but fundamentally by your effort, and this means by your facing the things you fear. RECOVERY LIES IN THE PLACES AND EXPERIENCES FEARED.

Facing also means not shying away from nervous symptoms *for fear of making them worse*. Shying away is running away, not facing.

I met a striking example of not facing in a Canadian who panicked when away from home and who was consequently afraid to travel any distance from home, either alone or accompanied.

His therapist encouraged him to go out as far as he could without panicking. If he panicked (and he surely would), he was told to return home and repeat the journey later, still going only as far as he could with comfort. The therapist's aim was for the patient to become so used to that particular journey that he could eventually make it without panic.

This man managed so well, he decided to spend his

holiday in the United States. He spent two weeks in Las Vegas and did not panic. He returned home in triumph.

The next day he went down to his bank; the same bank he had visited so often when ill. He stood on the old familiar spot in the queue, and as he handed his bank-book to the same teller – the one with the thick-rimmed glasses – memory smote and he panicked. *And this time it was a smasher*, because with the return of panic came despair. He had managed so well before going away, and yet all he need do now was simply stand in the queue in his own bank for panic to sweep once more. No wonder he despaired and thought, 'What can I do *now*?' He was desolate.

He had found peace only by getting-used-to. He had never faced panic, had never learned how to cope with it fully. He had been taught to avoid it, to try to quieten it, never how to pass through it until *it no longer mattered*.

It is true that some people feel they have been helped by avoiding, but *they are vulnerable to returns of panic*. At the return of even a slight spasm, their brave little flag can crumple.

I stress again, and again, that in place of an inner voice that says hopefully, 'Perhaps it won't happen here,' there must be a supporting voice that says, 'It doesn't matter if it *does* happen here. It just doesn't matter any more. You can cope with it!' The voice that says, 'Perhaps it won't ... ?' is the sword of Damocles, waiting.

While I never teach the 'getting-used-to' technique to people afraid of travelling away from home, it has its place in treating people with specific phobias, such as fear of cats, thunderstorms, heights and so on. Behaviourists build a program of graduated exposure to a feared object that can not only relieve, but often cure this kind of phobia.

Also, it is possible to get so used to some nervous symptoms that they no longer matter. Then without the stress of mattering, they may, of course, calm, even disappear.

I also said facing means accepting that cure must come from within oneself and not from some permanent outside crutch. This means recognising that the way to recovery can be difficult. A journalist wrote in a magazine that she had been agoraphobic for years, but could now go anywhere providing she took a special tablet three times a day. 'Now,' she wrote, 'I have only to come off the tablets and I am cured!' She had only to stop taking medicine! In other words, while still lame, she had only to throw away her crutches and walk.

Whether she could do this would depend on her luck the first time she tried to go out without her tablets. If she was confident, and stayed confident, all could be well, but she needed only a slight shiver of doubt for panic to strike and all could be lost. This applies to the return of all the symptoms of nervous illness, when suppressed by medication. This merely postpones the time when symptoms must be faced to be cured. There is a place for medication but it should be chosen with discretion. I talk more about this later.

The permanent cure of nervous illness based on fear of symptoms and experiences – as so much nervous illness is –

begins by facing fear itself, especially at the peak of its intensity, THE RIGHT WAY.

While facing fear blindly is brave, it is too often futile and exhausting. For recovery, the sufferer must be shown how to face fear by *accepting*, *floating* and *letting time pass*.

12. Accepting

After becoming prepared to face, the next step is acceptance, and as acceptance is the key to recovery we should be sure of its meaning. Acceptance means letting the body loosen as much as possible and then going toward, not withdrawing from, the feared symptoms, the feared experiences. It means 'letting go', 'going with', bending like the willow before the wind – rolling with the punches!

When one goes forward this way into panic (into any of the feared symptoms), the secretion of the hormones (principally adrenalin) producing the symptoms is reduced. Even if only slightly, *it is reduced*. On the other hand, tense withdrawal encourages further secretion and so more sensitisation, and therefore more intense symptoms.

While at first acceptance of physical symptoms, especially panic, may seem impossible, practising thinking about acceptance is always possible and this alone can release some tension (although perhaps only a microscopic amount to begin with), so that when 'it' comes to do its worst, the worst is tempered. If you stand taut and say bravely with clenched teeth, 'Come and do your worst! But get it over quickly!' you are only putting-up-with.

A patient will complain that he has accepted but that the dreaded symptoms are still there. 'I have accepted the churning in my stomach but I still have it! So what do I do now?' How could he have accepted, while he still complained about it?

The most frightening symptom is panic because, in a sensitised person, it can strike so fiercely and so quickly, merely thinking about it apprehensively can bring it on. The natural reaction is to recoil; however, tension brings more sensitisation and so, more panic. Acceptance is a definite physiological process that eventually soothes. I say eventually, because the soothing can rarely be felt immediately. Acceptance is the beginning. Established sensitisation can rarely be soothed quickly, because it takes time for the new mood of acceptance to be felt as peace.

Although the symptoms of nervous illness are always the expression of mood, they are not always an expression of the present mood. When acceptance is first practised, the body may still be registering the tense, frightened mood of the preceding weeks, months, years, and may continue to do this (but with progressively reduced intensity) even after the mood of acceptance is established.

This is why nervous illness can be so puzzling. A nervously ill person may begin to accept, but when the symptoms do not quickly disappear, he loses heart and becomes apprehensive once more, although trying to convince himself that he is still accepting.

I repeat, it takes time for a body to establish acceptance and for this to bring peace, just as it takes time for fear to be established as continuous tension and anxiety. This is why letting time pass, the last of my four concepts, is so important in treatment.

Understanding makes acceptance so much easier. It is unnecessarily difficult to accept erratic heartbeats if the victim believes that her heart is diseased. How much easier when she understands that the unevenness of those beats is no more than a temporary and unimportant upset in their nervous timing.

Adequate explanation is indeed a boon to the patient preparing to accept. However, it is not always given. One woman said, 'I can't describe how I feel. I just feel funny. The doctors just look at me and give no explanation!'

'Feeling funny' can be an accurate description of how a nervously ill person does sometimes feel and describing her 'funny' symptoms can be difficult, because symptoms of fatigue and anxiety when working together can be vague, undefined, and vague symptoms can be just as upsetting as more definite ones.

If you feel like this, providing your doctor has examined you and said that your 'funny' symptoms are nervous, accept them and be comforted to know that funny feelings are common in nervous illness and never important. Blind acceptance can cure as well as acceptance based on knowledge; but when knowledge guides, acceptance is easier.

Some doctors, while knowing that 'funny' symptoms are 'nervous', do not understand their physiology and so cannot explain them. So, while 'funny' nervous feelings should be accepted without full explanation (if none is available), explanation of more definite symptoms (weakness, trembling, headache, palpitations, difficulty in swallowing and so on) should be sought. I explain these in detail later in the book.

Don't think I use the word acceptance lightly. I know what I am asking. It's not easy to accept the fire that consumes; not easy to work with the fire burning. It's not easy to accept and work with a body that feels as if it is vibrating, shaking; with stomach churning, limbs aching, heart pounding, sight blurred, head swimming . . . I'm making it sound terrible, aren't I? It can be terrible and it is made worse if the mind, at the same time, feels as if it is drawn out into a frail thread that will snap with the slightest extra tension. I understand all this, but I still preach acceptance.

One day a woman phoned to say that that morning had been especially rough for her. She'd come through by saying to herself, 'I'll be talking to Dr Weekes in a couple of hours. I'll have some peace then!' The thought of the peace to come sustained her. But living for such peaceful moments was not good enough; it meant that she would make little progress. There is no lasting peace in waiting for someone else to bring it. Such relief from suffering is only a respite.

I explained to this woman that peace lay within herself, and depended on her attitude when the symptoms were at their fiercest, and that that was the moment for her to practise the acceptance that would help her find lasting peace.

She thought for a while and then said, 'You mean I have to find the eye of the hurricane!' She had the message at last. Sailors say that at the centre of the hurricane there is a place of peace which they call the 'eye'. The storm swirls around but cannot reach it. To find it the ship must first go through the storm.

If that woman were to work as willingly as possible, accepting the symptoms (the hurricane) and not add second-fear, she would find the eye of the storm herself, and although the symptoms may at first seem as fierce as ever, there would be some peace and reassurance in knowing that she was on the right course at last, without having to wait for the doctor's soothing words.

Peace of mind built on earned confidence lies not in the absence of symptoms but in their midst, and it is only when one discovers this that the intensity of symptoms abates and there is peace. The process, of course, is gradual. The next day the woman reported that while feeling 'ghastly', she had sat at her work (she was an artist) and had painted for two hours. For the first time for months she was able to lose herself in the work, while the hurricane raged within. For once, the hurricane did not seem so important.

It takes courage to face the storm and let happen what will. That woman had been shrinking from the way she felt for twenty years and was still ill. Surely it was time she tried another approach; tried to go into the storm, accepting it willingly – well, as willingly as she could manage at first.

Many are helped by understanding that the flash of panic is no more than an electrical discharge; that while it may feel devastating, it is only an electrical discharge along sensory nerves. SO MANY PEOPLE ALLOW AN ELECTRIC FLASH TO SPOIL THEIR LIVES BY WITHDRAWING FROM IT IN FEAR.

As I have explained so often, fearful withdrawal produces the hormones that stoke the fire of panic. Facing and relaxing toward, with acceptance, help to dampen the flow and eventually stop it.

A sensitised, bewildered person, feeling his panic grow stronger as his sensitisation increases, may imagine being flooded by an irresistible tidal wave of panic. If he analyses his fiercest flash – the flash he thinks too fierce to bear – he will find that at its peak, *he is shudderingly withdrawing from it.*

WHENEVER HE FEARS PANIC HE CAN EVENTUALLY QUELL IT ONLY BY GOING FORWARD INTO IT, NEVER BY WITHDRAWING FROM IT.

A person sustained by this knowledge will one day be surprised by feeling panic sweep over him and yet FEEL ALOOF FROM IT, as if looking down on it. HE HAS LOST HIS FEAR OF PANIC. We talk about 'rising above a situation'; there is no better example.

When there is no longer fear of panic, it gradually subsides. Time becomes the healer. I stress again, and again, that cure lies in losing fear and that this is earned only by learning how to go through it the right way – with acceptance. With such understanding, it is possible to be cured immediately. I have seen this – but, of course, rarely.

Repeated panics can be exhausting. This is when I advise moderate and temporary drug therapy and an occasional rest to help the sufferer regain strength and refresh his spirit.

Medication must always be planned so that the sufferer still earns his inner supporting voice born from having faced and accepted.

I talk so much about panic, because I am using it as an example from a hierarchy of nervous symptoms: palpitations, churning stomach, trembling hands and so on. When the sufferer learns to accept these without adding second-fear, they also gradually subside. They must, because they too are the symptoms of fear.

You may ask, 'But what if the nervously ill person is kept constantly stressed, perhaps frightened, by some problem – perhaps an upsetting domestic situation that is difficult to change? How can accepting the nervous symptoms help him? It can't solve the problem!'

It can't. However, people who develop nervous symptoms because of the stress brought by a problem, can also be further upset by the symptoms themselves; the iron-band headache, extreme fatigue, quickly beating heart, sweating hands and so on. Surely, understanding the nature of these symptoms helps lessen fear of them and so gives greater opportunity to concentrate on trying to solve any problem.

If you are reading this because you are nervously ill, I want you to practise acceptance now. Make yourself comfortable, take a deep breath, let it out slowly, let your tummy muscles sag, give way and try to feel a willingness to accept. Try to feel this in the pit of your stomach. Practise now.

Did you have a fleeting feeling of acceptance? If you did, you felt the birth of recovery. Continued acceptance will gradually finish the job.

It is necessary to understand the difference between true acceptance and putting-up-with. Putting-up-with (although calling for much bravery) means resistance. It means advancing and retreating at the same time. As I said earlier, it is an attitude of 'Hurry! Come quickly and get it over!'. True acceptance means facing and relaxing, being prepared to go slowly with as little self-induced agitation as possible. It is submission.

I have used acceptance again and again in writing and recordings. You may think I place too much importance on it. How could I when it is the key to recovery?

I have said so often that peace lies on the other side of panic: now I shout it. By going through panic to the other side you earn the little voice that says, 'It doesn't matter any more if panic comes!' This is the only voice to listen to. It is your staff, and will always come to your help in setbacks, even if you find yourself almost helpless on the floor. As it lifts you up, you will feel again that the dreaded bogey no longer matters. As this realisation strengthens, courage returns and you once more find the confidence to practise utter, utter acceptance – perhaps even more willingly.

Acceptance means throwing away the gun and letting the tiger come if he wants to. It sounds terrible, doesn't it? Incredible that cure can lie in such a dangerous procedure; but it does.

Just as facing and accepting are closely related, so are acceptance and floating. Indeed, they are so close that sometimes distinguishing between them is difficult.

Let us now examine floating.

13. Floating

In the past, orthodox psychiatric treatment rarely recognised the importance of fear-of-fear and too often persisted with searching for childhood causes, which was neither necessary nor helpful.

One woman wrote, 'Not one psychiatrist, or psychologist, I visited would listen to the validity of the "fear-of-the-fear" and yet I am living proof of it. They were like stone and you can't reason with stone.'

So, disappointed and confused, perhaps made apathetic with heavy medication, nervously ill people often abandon treatment and, with little hope, sink further into their illness. Some try to treat themselves.

Unfortunately, self-treatment often fails because instinct too readily leads the sufferer in the wrong direction. He tries to *fight* his illness. HE SHOULD FLOAT, NOT FIGHT.

Many ask, 'What do you mean exactly by floating, doctor?' I can explain best by giving examples. A nervously sensitised person can become so supertensed with fear that he may stand immobilised, rigid, feeling unable to take another step forward, whether trying to walk along a street, enter a shop, or simply go from room to room at home. He rarely recognises this 'paralysis' as supertension. Indeed, *his instinct is to tense himself still further and try to force his way forward.*

Forcing means more tension and therefore more rigidity. In his despair he may add panic to panic and when he does, his thoughts may seem to recede (they may actually seem to squeeze up into the back of his head) and become 'frozen' until further thought seems impossible. His 'brain goes numb'.

Agoraphobic people know and dread this moment of rigid 'paralysis' when trying to move away from home, and fear of it has helped to keep thousands house-bound for years.

If the 'paralysed' sufferer, instead of forcing, were to let his body go as slack as possible (and actually feel as if it was sagging), then take a deep breath and exhale slowly while imagining himself *floating forward* without resistance – almost as if floating on a cloud or on water – he would release enough tension to loosen muscles and would be able to move forward, although maybe at first shakily, haltingly.

Just 'a touch' of agoraphobia Agoraphobia is no more than one aspect of an ordinary anxiety state. A person in an anxiety state may have rapidly beating heart, sweating hands, may feel weak, giddy and have flashes of panic which grow worse if he is out where he thinks he may be trapped, cannot escape and so may end by making a fool of himself before other people. Hence, he may avoid going out and mixing with people, especially in a confined situation (public hall, church and so on).

In my opinion this is the basis of most agoraphobia and is a natural sequence to an anxiety state. And since it is possible to be in a mild or severe anxiety state, it's also possible to have mild or severe agoraphobia. For example, some days a person may feel well enough to go out alone, even to the supermarket, and yet on another day feel unable to face the front door. That is mild agoraphobia. A severe agoraphobic never goes out alone and may even refuse to go if accompanied.

There are certainly grades of the agoraphobic phase of an anxiety state.

Another example of floating: a nervously ill person may wake in the morning feeling so tired he may shrink at the thought of the effort of getting out of bed, dressing, eating – indeed, of doing anything.

He may try to 'pull himself together' and this may seem so impossible that he sinks, defeated, back onto his bed. One woman said she felt like an ant looking at Everest.

Instead of seeing only grim effort ahead, she should think, 'Okay, I'll make the effort *as gently as I can*. I'll "go with it". I'll try to make no tense effort; I'll submit to it all, let it happen. I'm not going to fight my way through any of it. I'll stop struggling and try to let my body float up and out of it. I'll even float my clothes on.'

Can you appreciate the difference here between fighting and floating? Floating means no grim determination, no clenched teeth; as little 'pushing', forcing, as possible.

You may say, 'Floating is only relaxing!' It is certainly relaxing, but it is more than that; it is relaxing *with action*. One faces, relaxes and then floats on through.

Floating does not mean lying and gazing at the ceiling and thinking 'I don't have to make any effort, I'll give up the struggle. I'll just lie here on the bed for ever and do nothing!' That's relaxing all right! But it's not relaxing with action. And yet, *temporarily* 'doing nothing about it' can have a beneficial, refreshing effect – but only temporarily.

The sufferer practising letting his body float up from his fatigue has no need to search for a way to recovery. It is as if he steps aside from his body and lets it find its own way out of the maze. The body that so skilfully heals a physical wound without our direction can also heal sensitised nerves if given a chance and not hindered by inquisitive fingers picking at the scar. Float, don't pick.

Too often the same difficulties arise again and again in nervous illness and the repeated effort of fighting the same battle can make the sufferer feel too dispirited to go on searching for a way out. WHERE FIGHTING IS EXHAUSTING, FLOATING – BY REMOVING THE TENSION OF FORCING – MAKES REPEATED EFFORT LESS DAUNTING.

If, when learning to float, loosening a tense body may seem impossible, the supertensed person can at least *imagine* himself loosening. Even this works.

As I have already mentioned, people in an anxiety state can be grouped into those who have a special problem, or problems, causing illness and keeping them ill, and those whose only problem is finding a way to recovery from their distressing nervous state.

Those with the specific problem are not expected to float past it, although I have been quoted as having asked this of them. Expecting a bewildered, confused person to find his own answer to his problem is rarely good therapy. It can mean an unnecessarily long period of suffering because too often, through sensitisation and fatigue, the sufferer switches too easily and too quickly from one point of view to another. Holding one point of view that brings some peace is essential for recovery. A good therapist helps his or her patient find such a viewpoint.

It is rare to meet a nervously ill person who can float past an agitating problem and worry no more about it. I do say 'try to let all disturbing, obstructive thought float away, out of your head', but of course, success here depends on the magnitude of the troublesome thought. When I have given that advice previously, I have referred to floating past one's own destructive suggestion. I did not mean the nervously ill should try to float past real problems.

This is one patient's experience of facing, accepting and floating: 'I feel I must write and tell you of the progress I have made this year. For twenty years, since my first attack, I have been agoraphobic. During all these years, at the sight, or mere mention, of the word "bus", my stomach would turn over and the idea of getting on one – impossible.

'As you know, last year I got your cassette*, *Going on holiday* (your recordings are worn thin with playing). As a result of constantly listening to the cassette, I decided to face a short cruise for myself and family.

'This year I booked a much longer cruise (a month!) to the Canary Islands. So, it was on with the cassette again. The first four days were not so good. The sea was rough and there was a strong wind. However, I had made up my mind to do everything I have been unable to do for so long. I went six times in the coach to the restaurant *alone*. I went up the mountains at Tenerife, 4000 feet, with a sheer drop on either side. I even crossed to the shore by launch.

'Only one evening was spoilt. When I entered the dining room that night, I had a terrible feeling of self-consciousness. I just couldn't swallow and it was my favourite meal, roast turkey! I did the only thing I could think of: I ate the soft vegetables and the dessert and kept repeating to myself, "Loosen your body! Accept and float! Accept and float!" By the time we had reached the coffee I was floating fine.'

So now practise floating and while you do be prepared to obey the next section, and let time pass.

* For a full list of Dr Weekes' CDs and DVDs, and information on where to obtain them, see p.265.

14. Letting time pass

Recovery, like all healing, must be given time. Understandably the nervously ill person is impatient with time and wants immediate appeasement; but impatience means tension and tension is the enemy of healing.

The sufferer removes a big obstacle to recovery when he understands that sensitisation is a chemical process and needs time for chemical readjustment. A still sensitised body can be deceptively calm in a calm atmosphere but a body even only slightly sensitised cannot always maintain calmness when under renewed stress. So time, more time, must pass. Time itself is a healer. It's rather like the donkey and the carrot. The carrot (recovery) must be shifted just a little further forward during each setback but always remain within sight.

I am often asked how long recovery will take. So much depends on the degree of sensitisation and the circumstances of recovery. There may be constant strain; for example, trying to recover while living with an upsetting domestic situation. Also, it takes time to blunt memory's cutting edge. We can't anaesthetise memory. Indeed, when surprised by some gruelling memory, who can suppress an inner shudder? And yet, the person trying to recover from nervous illness seems to think he should. He wants the balm of constant peace.

It is difficult to understand that a body's sensitised reaction to memory is no more than the working of a natural law; difficult to understand that setback is not always a setback in the sense that it sets *back*, but should be even expected and accepted *as part of recovery*. Its victim is much more likely to believe that some strange jinx is bugging him. His jinx is his lack of understanding. When so close to past upsetting experiences, and with a body still tuned to give a too quick, too intense, reaction to memory's prodding, it is natural to be too easily bluffed by memory into thinking he will never recover.

When memory first strikes it is as if the sufferer has learned nothing from past experience. The symptoms he'd learned to disregard suddenly begin to matter again – very much. And before he has time to study himself enough to think clearly, he feels sucked willy-nilly into the whirlpool of setback. However, if he had originally worked his way out of suffering the hard way – by having truly faced and lived with his symptoms while accepting them, having conquered adding second-fear (fear of symptoms, especially fear of panic) – then memory of his original recovery gradually awakens the little inner voice that says, 'You've come out of it before. You can do it now! You know that these symptoms do not really matter!' He hears this voice with thanksgiving and relief, because with it comes a special feeling, a realisation that the symptoms really do *not* matter. He now *feels* this; doesn't just think it as he did at the beginning of setback. *He now feels it with relief.* Fear gradually goes; relaxation and peace come. He is on the way to true recovery. Recovery is built on repeated experiences of discovering that symptoms no longer matter.

When enough setbacks bring enough such experiences, the feeling of symptoms-no-longer-mattering comes more quickly, is more forceful, and the impact of memory's shock becomes weaker and weaker until it is but an echo of former suffering.

It is possibly because memory can shock by bringing back old symptoms so vividly that some therapists speak pessimistically about complete recovery. Indeed, they do not recognise that setback is one of the best teachers, and an almost essential halting place in recovery because it gives more time to relearn and practise. Not understanding this, they fail to prepare their patients optimistically for possible setback.

At some point in nervous illness the sufferer may be so ill he no longer cares what happens; however, as he begins to recover, caring returns and this may be complicated by his feeling that although much better, he cannot face the future demands and responsibilities of normal living. At such a time he is often accused of 'not wanting to get better'. Make no mistake, he wants to recover, but at the same time the prospect of coping with the demands of recovery may be so frightening while he is in his present state of only partial recovery, that he almost convinces himself that the criticism may be true – another bewilderment in nervous illness!

Enough time must pass to provide a protective layer of normal responses to help him gradually find his balance in normal living, to take normal reaction for granted.

As his body strengthens, his spirits rise, optimism and confidence return. The process may be so gradual he may be unaware of it. It is this gradualness that makes all possible and only the passage of enough time can bring such gradualness.

A Dutchman once said to Vera Brittain (an English author) that the postwar Dutch were suffering from a spiritual sickness which time and understanding alone would heal. He said that suffering could not be erased the moment the war ended and peace came; time was necessary for the Dutch to regain their balance, their ability to be on top of events, including their own lives. He added, 'Be patient with us. We have to grow into liberty.' And so must the nervously ill person grow into recovery. There is no electric switch, no overnight cure.

When the sufferer is beginning to recover, he is not only vulnerable to memory, but also is particularly vulnerable to the tricks any remaining fatigue may play. For example, distinguishing between normal fatigue and some remnant of nervous fatigue can baffle. The sufferer is apt to mistake any fatigue as nervous and jump to the upsetting conclusion that recovery is further away than he had thought. One woman, although much better, was so apprehensively suggestible that when she had made foolish mistakes playing bridge, she always blamed lingering illness and became worried. But she made foolish mistakes at bridge before she was ill! Many nervously ill people expect recovery to bring a state of peace they never previously felt.

As already mentioned, for many people peace is often further delayed by their too fearful, and too tense, recoil from a binding awareness of self – the result of months, even years, of concentration on themselves and their illness. They delay their own recovery by trying to force forgetfulness. *Nothing can be forced in nervous illness.* The only way to lose consciousness of self is to accept it; to accept any thought that comes as part of ordinary thinking. This means that they should think about themselves and their illness *as much as the habit demands* and realise that *it is only a habit fostered by mental fatigue.* Once more I stress that the key to recovery is not in *forgetting* but in *no-longer-mattering*, and for this, *time* must pass.

When the patient realises that the intensity of his reaction is part of his sensitisation and that if he accepts it and lets more time pass, those reactions will gradually become normal, then intense reaction can be borne more philosophically. This is sometimes called regaining one's balance and, as the Dutchman said to Vera Brittain, it takes time.

15. Cure of the more constant symptoms

First, look at yourself and notice how you are sitting in your chair. I have no doubt that you are tensely shrinking from the feelings within you and yet, at the same time, are ready to 'listen in' in apprehension. I want you to do *the exact opposite.* I want you to sit as comfortably as you can, relax to the best of your ability by letting your arms and legs sag into the chair as if charged with lead, and take slow, deep breaths through your partly opened mouth. Now examine and *do not shrink from* the sensations that have been upsetting you. I want you to examine each carefully, *to analyse and describe it aloud to yourself.* For example, you may say, 'My hands sweat, they tremble and feel sore . . .' This may sound a little silly and you may smile. So much the better.

CHURNING STOMACH

Begin with the nervous feeling in your stomach, the so-called churning. This may feel like an uneasy fluttering or may bore steadily like a hot poker passing from your stomach through your back. Do not tensely flinch from it. Go with it. Relax and analyse it. Take a few minutes to do this before reading further.

Now that you have faced and examined it, is it so terrible? If you had arthritis in your wrist, you would be prepared to work with the arthritic pain without becoming too upset. Why regard this churning as something so different from ordinary pain that it can frighten you? Stop regarding it as some monster trying to possess you. Understand that it is but the working of oversensitised adrenalin-releasing nerves and that by constantly shrinking from it you have stimulated an excessive outflow of adrenalin which has further excited your nerves to produce continual churning.

While you examine and analyse this churning a strange thing may happen: you may find your attention wandering from yourself. This 'thing' that seemed so terrible while you stayed tense and flinched from it, may fail to hold your attention for long when you see it for what it is – no more than a strange physical feeling of no great medical significance, and causing no real harm.

So, be prepared to accept and live with it for the time being. Accept it as something that will be with you for some time yet – in fact, while you recover – but something that will eventually leave you if you are prepared to let time pass and not anxiously watch the churning during its passing.

But do not make the mistake of thinking that it will go *as soon as you cease to fear it.* Your nervous system is still tired and will take time to heal, just as a broken leg takes time.

However, as you improve and are no longer afraid of the churning, and do not try to cure it by controlling it, and are prepared to accept it and work with it present, you will become more interested in other things and will gradually forget to notice whether it is there or not. *This is the way to recover*. By true acceptance you break the fear–adrenalin– fear cycle, or, in other words, the churning–adrenalin– churning cycle.

True acceptance

From this discussion you will appreciate that *true acceptance is the keystone to your recovery*, and before you continue with the examination of your other symptoms we should make sure that we understand its exact meaning.

I find that some patients complain, 'I have accepted the churning in my stomach, but it is still there. So what am I to do now?' How could they have accepted it while they still complain about it?

Or, as one old man said, 'After breakfast the churning starts. I can't just sit there and churn. If I do, I'm exhausted after an hour, so I have to get up and walk around. But I'm too tired to walk round, so what am I to do?' I said to him, 'You haven't really accepted that churning, have you?' 'Oh, yes I have,' he answered indignantly. 'I'm not frightened of it any more.'

But he obviously was. He was afraid that after an hour's churning he would be exhausted, so he sat tensely dreading its arrival, shrinking from it when it came and worrying about the exhaustion to follow. Of course, the churning, itself a symptom of tension, *must inevitably come while so tensely awaited.*

I tried to make him understand that he must be prepared to *let his stomach churn* and to continue reading his paper without dwelling on the churning. *Only by so doing would he be truly accepting.* In this way, and only in this way, would he eventually reach the stage when *it would no longer matter whether his stomach churned or not.* Then, freed from the stimulus of tension and anxiety, his adrenalin-releasing nerves would gradually calm down and *the churning would automatically lessen and finally cease.*

This man was asked to do no more than change his mood from apprehension to acceptance. *The symptoms of this type of breakdown are always a reflection of your mood.* However, it is well to remember that it may be some time before your body reacts to the new mood of acceptance and that it may continue for a while to reflect the tense, frightened mood of the preceding weeks, months or years. This is one reason why nervous breakdown can be so bewildering and why this old man was bewildered. He had begun to accept, but when the symptoms did not disappear immediately, he quickly lost heart and became apprehensive again, although trying to convince himself that he was accepting. It takes time for a body to establish acceptance as a mood and for this eventually to bring peace just as it took time for fear to become established as continuous tension and anxiety. That is why 'letting time pass' is such an important part of your treatment and why I shall emphasise it again and again. Time is the answer. *But there must be that background of true acceptance while waiting for time to pass.*

SWEATING, TREMBLING HANDS

Now look at your hands. They sweat? Maybe tremble? Maybe the skin is sore and tingles with 'pins and needles'? But the hands of any tense, frightened person may feel like that, and you are certainly frightened, so how could your hands behave otherwise? The sweating, trembling, 'pins and needles' and soreness are no more than the physical expression of *over-sensitisation of your adrenalin-releasing nerves through anxiety and fear.* These sensations get no worse than this and could never prevent you using your hands. Maybe your hands do sweat and tremble, but *they are still good hands to use.*

Therefore, accept the sweating, trembling, soreness and tingling for the time being. These cannot be cured overnight. With acceptance, although your hands may still tremble and sweat for a while, you will find some peace, enough to begin to still the outflow of adrenalin, so that your sweat glands will gradually calm down. In place of fear–adrenalin–sweat, you put acceptance–less adrenalin–less sweat; and finally you have peace–no excess adrenalin–no excess sweat. It is as simple as that, although acceptance may not seem so simple at first.

Hyperthyroidism

Hot, trembling hands are also found in a sickness called hyperthyroidism, which is not 'just nerves', although it looks very much like it, and which must be treated specifically. Do not persevere with hot, trembling hands unless you have the assurance of your doctor that you do not have hyperthyroidism. Once given such assurance, accept it and do not waste time and energy worrying for fear the doctor may have made a mistake. If you cannot accept his assurance, seek a second opinion but do not inquire beyond that. Hyperthyroidism is usually not difficult to diagnose.

RACING HEART OR HEART 'SHAKES'

Now examine your racing heart. By 'racing' I do not mean the short attacks of palpitation you may have from time to time, but the constantly quickly beating, thumping, banging, 'shaking' heart that is your daily companion. You probably think it is racing, that is why I chose this expression, but if you find a watch with a second hand and take your pulse, I doubt if it will be beating at more than one hundred beats each minute. It may be beating at one hundred and twenty, but I doubt it. In fact, your heart is probably not working much harder than any other healthy heart. The difference is that you have become *sensitised to its beating so that you feel each beat.* And you will remain sensitised to its beating while you listen to and anxiously record each beat!

I want you to realise that it will not harm your heart in the least to beat this way. You could play tennis or baseball if you wished. In fact, if you had the interest and energy to play such games, it is most likely that your heart would calm down and beat more slowly while you were playing than when you are sitting holding your pulse. I am assuming, of course, that you have had a medical examination and have been told that your trouble is 'only nerves'.

These weeks of watching, waiting and holding your pulse have been a waste of time. You cannot harm your heart. You can do anything you wish, provided you are prepared to put up temporarily with the strange feelings that come from the region of your heart. The soreness and pain are merely muscular chest-wall strain, brought on by tension. A diseased heart does not register pain where you feel it. *Heart pain proper is not felt in the heart.*

So, as far as your heart is concerned, it is a good heart, beating very much like any other. You are only aware of its beating and are making yourself more aware by worrying about it and paying it too much attention. Have the courage to relax and analyse this beating and understand that it, too, like the sweating hands and churning stomach, is once again the result of oversensitisation of adrenalin-releasing nerves. The nerves of your heart have become so sensitised by fear that they answer the slightest stimulus. A sudden noise may suffice to make your heart 'rattle'; or, more puzzling still, it may suddenly beat quickly for no apparent reason.

Be prepared to live with this erratic beating until your nerves become less sensitised. They will do this as you become more philosophical and accept the racing and thumping as part of your recovery program. You have made the mistake of thinking that while your heart continued to beat quickly, you must still be ill. It may be some weeks before you cease to be conscious of the quick action, but once you accept it, *you will be getting better all the time.*

There is no magic switch to immediately calm your heart, although medication can be a great help and you need not hesitate to let your doctor prescribe it.

SORE HEAD

The soreness around, or on top of, your head is caused by contraction of your scalp muscles as a result of continuous tension. You may notice how relief comes if you press your scalp or place a hot water-bottle where it is most sore. This should prove to you that the cause is local, where you can reach it, and is not deep-seated. *These are not the symptoms of brain tumour.*

Since contraction of tense muscle causes pain, it naturally becomes worse when you worry and improves as you relax and release tension. Pain-killing tablets help, but only a little. With the relaxation that follows acceptance, tension eases and the pain gradually lessens. However, this scalp pain, this 'iron band', is a most stubborn symptom to cure, so do not despair if it lingers a while. I assure you that it eventually goes. The hardest, tightest band will gradually lessen and disappear with acceptance.

Once more, true acceptance

Make sure that you appreciate the difference between truly accepting and only thinking you are accepting. If you can let your stomach churn, your hands sweat, your heart thump quickly, and your head ache, without paying too much attention to them, then you are truly accepting. It does not matter so much if at first you cannot do this calmly. It may be impossible to be calm at this stage. All I ask for true acceptance is that you are *prepared to live and work with your symptoms without paying them too much respect.*

The limited power of adrenalin-releasing nerves

After examining these 'terrible feelings', I want you to remain seated and concentrate on each in turn and try to make it worse. You will find you cannot. Apparently *the power of the adrenalin-releasing nerves is limited.* You may succeed in slightly intensifying its effect with concentration, but only slightly. And yet, all this time, without realising it, you have been shrinking from facing these symptoms squarely because you were afraid that by so doing you would somehow make them worse. It was as if you gave them a fearful, sideways glance.

Let me reassure you. You cannot increase your symptoms by facing them or even trying to intensify them. In fact, you may find that when you try consciously to make them worse, they improve. The very act of concentrating on them in this way means that, for the time being at least, you look at them with interest rather than fear, and even this brief respite from tension may have a calming effect. *Symptoms can be intensified only by further fear and its resulting tension, never by relaxing, facing and accepting.* Are you beginning to suspect that your symptoms may have had you bluffed? They most certainly have.

A student whose sensations were very much as I have described, could make little headway at his study because of banging heart, sweating hands and churning stomach. One day, when he thought he would go crazy unless he could get relief, a friend, an ex-soldier, came to see him. He told his friend about his suffering and said, 'I can't stand it much longer. I have done all I can to fight it and I don't know which way to turn next. Surely there is a way out of this hell?'

The friend explained that many soldiers at the 'front' had had nerves like this until they realised they were only being bluffed by them. He advised the youth to stop being bluffed by his nerves, to float past all suggestion of self-pity and fear and go on with his work. The student saw the light and from being afraid to put one foot in front of the other for fear of damaging his heart, in two weeks was climbing mountains. That was many years ago. He has similar feelings from time to time when overwrought but he knows that they will pass if he relaxes, accepts and floats past them. He has learned how to live with his nerves.

'FLOATING' NOT 'FIGHTING'

To float is just as important as to accept, and it works similar magic. I could say let 'float' and not 'fight' be your slogan, because it amounts to that.

Let me illustrate more clearly the meaning of float in this regard. A patient had become so afraid of meeting people that she had not entered a shop for months. When asked to make a small purchase she said, 'I couldn't go into a shop. I've tried, but I can't. The harder I try, the worse I get. If I force myself, I feel I am paralysed and can't put one foot in front of the other. So please don't ask me to go into a shop.'

I told her that she had little hope of succeeding while she tried to force herself in this way. This was the fighting of which I had previously warned her. I explained that she must imagine she was floating into the shop, not fighting her way there. To make this easier, she could imagine she was actually on a cloud, floating through the door. I also explained that she could further help herself by letting any obstructive thought she might have float away out of her head, recognising that it was no more than a thought and that she need not be bluffed into giving it attention.

When she came back she was overjoyed and said, 'Don't stop me. I'm still floating. Do you want me to float for something else?'

Strange, isn't it, how the use of one simple word could free a mind that had been imprisoned for months? The explanation is simple enough. When you fight you become tense and tension inhibits action. *When you think of floating you relax and this helps action.* This woman was in such a state of tension that I have seen her nearly reduced to tears when, with shaking hands, she tried to find a car key in her handbag. After learning to float, one day when on a similar search she said, 'Sorry if I'm taking your time. The keys can't be too far away. I've just floated past two bills, a lipstick and a purse. I'll float round a bit longer and find them.' The shaking hands were almost steady. She was learning to float past tension.

I have seen patients so tensed by continuous fear that they were convinced they could neither walk nor lift their arms to feed themselves. One man afflicted in this way had been bedridden for weeks. After a few conversations with him, I found he was able to understand that the paralysis lay in his thoughts and not in his muscles. He learned the trick of freeing his muscles by *floating past obstructive thought*. Within a few days he was 'floating' the food to his mouth unaided and announced that he was now ready to walk.

This caused a fine stir in the ward. Several doctors, students and nurses stood by to watch. No sooner had the patient stood up than a nurse, seeing him sway, said hurriedly, 'Look out – you might fall!'

The patient, describing the event afterwards, said that this suggestion was almost too much, and he nearly crumpled to the floor. However, he heard a voice in the background saying, 'Float and you can do it. Float past fear,' and, he said, 'I "floated" down the hospital ward and back, to my own and everyone else's astonishment.'

Such frightening thoughts as were experienced by these two people can be very persistent, almost obsessive, to a tired mind, and it helps some people to imagine a pathway along which they can let these thoughts escape, float away. (Another use for 'float'.) For example, one woman thought of them as passing out of the back of her head; another said she let them float away along a channel over her right ear, where the grocer keeps his pencil; yet another thought of them as little balls that she let bounce off her head. This may sound childish to a healthy, resilient mind, capable of directing and discarding thought, but to the exhausted, frightened person it is not childish. Nothing that helps is childish to him, and this idea works well.

The first panic 'The first time I panicked was out shopping in Exeter. I'd had a cup of tea in the store and had gone up to the powder room. I felt so panicky I asked to be taken home. That experience so upset me, I didn't go to Exeter for ages.

'I panicked again three weeks later. I was tense at the time, having been to the dentist a few days earlier; a set appointment always worries me. Just two days later came my grand-daughter's christening. It was a lovely service in a delightful church and I enjoyed it very much. There was a buffet meal afterwards at a local hotel. I enjoyed watching the people looking after my mother (she was eighty-five) and helping my eighteen-month-old grand-daughter with her meal. I got chocolate on my hands and decided to wash them.

'I know the hotel well but the powder room is newly built and strange. It was empty when I got there. I can see now the connection between the panic in Exeter and the panic on this occasion. The trouble started when I locked the toilet door. I always find locking doors threatening. First comes the fear and then everything seems to recede. I know what I am and what I am doing but I seem to be in a dream, to have lost my identity. I remember at Exeter wondering if I was still alive. In the middle of all this, I remembered Dr Weekes saying, "Take no notice of strange feelings. Loosen and accept!"

'I washed my hands and they took ages to dry under the dryer. I looked in the mirror. I felt awful and

I looked awful, and thought, "I'll do my hair and powder my nose and then go back." This I did. I then went back along the corridor to the dining room, sat down and carried on where I had left off. The feeling of panic had almost subsided.

'The next day I was very tired but I decided that I would not be put out by it this time although I kept remembering it.

'Doctor, had the feeling reached its peak or could it have got worse? Was it likely to have lasted any longer? If that was "it", I know I can cope with it again should it recur.'

To wish for reassurance that 'it' could grow no greater shows that this woman still fears panic and while she is afraid she harbours the seeds of further panic. For her, 'it' certainly could have got worse had she not coped the way she did. She must try not to rest secure in the feeling 'I can stand *that* much!' She must know that *she can face and go through panic however fiercely it may come.* She can have this comfort: even the fiercest flash has its limit! Only when she can pass through any flash the right way will she lose fear of both 'it' and the menacing shadow of 'perhaps!'.

Panic takes many strange forms and 'recession' is one of them. I have already mentioned it in this book. Recession is a feeling of thoughts going back, back, right to the very back of the head; frightening, because the sufferer wonders if he will ever come back to be himself again. Recession is no more than tension's screws clamping more tightly than usual – a feeling of being encased in one's own mind – identity lost! It is essential to recognise and not be bluffed by tension's strange tricks. The calmness that comes with the relaxation (even the slightest) that understanding brings (it came to this woman to some extent when she remembered my words and returned to her friends) helps to unclamp the clamp. There is nothing to fear.

Masterly inactivity

Masterly inactivity, a well-known phrase, is another way to describe floating. It means to give up the struggle, to stop holding tensely onto yourself trying to control your fear, trying 'to do something about it' while subjecting yourself to constant self-analysis. It means to cease trying to navigate your way out of breakdown by meeting each obstacle as if it were a challenge that must be met before recovery is possible. It means to by-pass the struggle, to go around, not over the mountain, to float and let time pass.

The average person, tense with battling, has an innate aversion to practising masterly inactivity and letting go. He vaguely thinks that were he to do this, he would lose control over the last vestige of his will-power and his house of cards would tumble. As one young man said, 'I feel I must stand on guard. If I were to let go, I'm sure something would snap. It is absolutely necessary for me to keep control and hold myself together.' When he was obliged to talk to strangers, he would dig his nails into his palms while he tried to control his trembling body and conceal his state of nervous tension. He would watch the clock anxiously, wondering how much longer he could keep up this masquerade without 'cracking'.

Loosen your attitude

It is especially to such tense, controlled, nail-biting people that I say 'practise masterly inactivity and let go'. If your body trembles, *let it tremble*. Don't feel obliged to try and stop it. Don't try to appear normal. Don't even strive for relaxation. Simply let the thought of relaxation be in your mind, in your attitude toward your body. Loosen your attitude. In other words, *don't be too concerned because you are tense and cannot relax.* The very act of being prepared to accept your tenseness relaxes your mind, and relaxation of body gradually follows. *You don't have to strive for relaxation. You have to wait for it.* When a patient says, 'I have tried so hard all day to be relaxed,' surely he has had a day of striving, not relaxation? *Let your body find its own level without controlling, directing it.* Believe me, if you do this, you will not crack. You will not lose true control of yourself. You will float up to the surface from the depths of despair.

The relief of loosening your tense hold on yourself, of giving up the struggle and recognising that there is no battle to fight, except of your own making, may bring a calmness you have forgotten existed within you. In your tense effort to control yourself you have been releasing more and more adrenalin and so further exciting your organs to produce the very sensations from which you have been trying to escape.

So:

- Float past tension and fear.
- Float past unwelcome suggestions.
- Float, don't fight.
- Accept and let more time pass.

16. Cure of recurring nervous attacks

Now let us consider the symptoms of breakdown that may occur in attacks – panic spasms, palpitations, slowly beating heart, 'missed' heartbeats, trembling turns, inability to take a deep breath, 'lump in the throat', giddiness, nausea and vomiting. Depression and sleeplessness are such an important part of the nervous breakdown caused by problem, sorrow, guilt or disgrace, that in order to save repetition I shall leave their discussion until describing this second type of breakdown.

PANIC SPASMS

As already mentioned, fear can produce a state of constant tension, or it can take the form of intense recurring spasms of panic that start in our 'middle', just below the breast-bone, and seem to spread, like a white-hot flame, all over the body, passing through the chest, up the spine, into the face, down the arms and even down into the groins to the tips of the toes.

If you suffer from these spasms you will probably find that whereas you had some control over them at the beginning of your breakdown, you now seem to have lost control and live in constant dread of them. Your nervous system has become so sensitised to them that it discharges them instantly and swiftly at the slightest provocation. In this sensitised state you remain tense with an apprehension which helps only to increase the frequency and intensity of the spasms. Can you see the vicious circle in which you have placed yourself?

The treatment already offered to cure the symptoms of sustained fear will also cure these spasms of acute fear. You *face, analyse and try to understand them, learning how to live with them temporarily, letting time pass to bring recovery.*

In the past, as soon as you have felt a wave of panic approaching, you have either tried to control it and stop it coming or have shrunk from it and tried to forget it as quickly as possible. In this way you have lived in constant dread, preparing a battleground for each approaching spasm. Now, just as you examined and described your churning stomach and sweating hands, on the next occasion when you panic I want you to examine this feeling without shrinking from it, describing it to yourself as it sweeps through you.

You find that *fear strikes hardest when it first strikes*, and that if you relax and stand your ground and see it through, it quietens and disappears. When you have learned the trick of relaxing and seeing the wave of fear through to its finish *without adding further panic and tension to fear*, or *without trying to arrest it by controlling it*, you will begin *to lose your fear of fear*. You will probably be surprised to realise that a hot feeling in your stomach, a burning feeling up your spine, pins and needles in your hands and a throbbing feeling in your temples could have held such terror for you. *You have been terrified of no more than a physical feeling*. By analysing fear in this way and seeing it as a physical feeling that conforms to a set pattern and disappears with acceptance and relaxation, YOU UNMASK FEAR AND WITH IT YOUR OWN BREAKDOWN, AND YOU FIND THAT ONLY A BOGEY REMAINS.

Super-panic. Hanging on to a lamp-post for support

'I have super-panics. I feel faint, dizzy, can't breathe properly and I'm going to collapse. I've even hung on to lamp-posts for support. On top of this, I feel as though I'm "not there" and that I'm not going to come out of this terrible thing.

'How can I stop this sort of panic from coming on? I do *stay* on the bus, or walk down the street. I've tried to do what you've taught me, but when a panic is as bad as this, how can you expect people to let it come and carry on with what they're doing? Also, I'm drained when I've had an attack; I feel so weak and humiliated, how can I stay calm? I'm sure I'm about to die and I run for any escape I can see at the time.'

This is a striking example of what agoraphobia is all about. Every symptom this woman mentions comes from extreme fear, even terror, and she has put herself into this state because of her fear of the symptoms of fear. She is in a cycle of the symptoms of fear creating more fear.

Unfortunately, a very brave woman has got herself into this impasse by thinking she was accepting when she was only putting-up-with. I appreciate fully how difficult becoming unafraid of panic is while its lash is so scorching. Small wonder so many despair. The lash can be so severe, the spirit seems to collapse beneath it.

While it is possible to take the severest flash without drug therapy (and many do), I do not expect every sufferer to do so. A rest from practising with temporary medication can give respite from suffering and help spirits rise until the sufferer is once more ready to face the tiger. After such respite he can let panic flash without crumpling so abjectly before it.

In my practice I would ask such a person (usually on the telephone) to tell me what she believed I wanted her to do. I insisted that she put her idea of acceptance into her own words until I was sure she knew the difference between it and putting-up-with.

I would ask her to try and feel acceptance right in her 'middle'. When she thought she did, I would say, 'Now walk down the street and hope you will panic so that you can practise accepting.'

So often a most relieved woman (or man) would return and say, 'I did it, doctor!' If she didn't 'make it' on that attempt, she usually did on the next. At least, we both persevered until she did.

I stress that there is a great difference between temporarily taking medication for a short respite while in a state of super-sensitisation and depending on it as a permanent crutch.

Attacks of panic usually decrease in severity, and number, following a pattern. The person practising acceptance passes gradually from being terrified and dreading panic, to disliking it; then from disliking, to finding it no longer mattering. This does not mean that panic no longer comes. It takes time for no-longer-mattering to bring no panic. It is important to realise that panic can still flash and no longer matter. This is the beginning of recovery.

Please, please don't withdraw in terror from the symptoms of terror. There is no way out in withdrawal.

I know that some therapists either accompany, or provide people who will accompany, their agoraphobic patients until they can travel comfortably away from home. However, in my opinion, *these people are left vulnerable to returns of panic*.

I know mine is the hard way to be cured, but if we are to talk of permanent cure, then we talk of my way. For permanent cure, a sufferer must learn to cope with his symptoms by learning to become unafraid of them. He must not be led gently until he gets used to being away from the safety of home. *There is no*

permanent cure in getting used to being in a certain
place so that panic does not come.

If your heart fails when you read this, and you think
that you could never practise what I teach, let it fail as
much as it likes, but know that there is nobody who
cannot practise this way if they make up their mind to
do it.

Other ways to conquer fear

There are ways to conquer fear other than analysing and
unmasking it, and some doctors have the experience of
watching a sufferer inventing her own method. Some find
the cause of the fear and try to conquer and control this,
believing that with the cause removed the fear will go. For
example, one woman, terrified of the palpitations because
of fear of dying during an attack, so succeeded in losing
her fear of death that she lost her fear of the palpitations.
I have not suggested that you use this method for this type
of breakdown, because there are too many instances where
much would be made from nothing and one difficulty
overcome only to find a dozen in its place. At this stage I
prefer to attack fear itself.

For example, Mrs G. was afraid to walk up the street to go
shopping. When she analysed why she was afraid, she found
many obstacles causing fear, among them passing the
telephone booth where she once collapsed, passing the
neighbour with the glittering eye, waiting to be served at the
butcher's, and so on – the list was long. To discover why she

feared each obstacle would have been a research program in itself. Common sense rebels at the thought. It is more satisfactory to find a common approach to meet each obstacle encountered on that journey up the street. Unmasking fear itself is such an approach. No longer afraid of the physical sensation of fear, Mrs G. can float past the telephone booth, past the neighbour's glittering eye, even into the butcher's.

While this method is excellent for minor fears, major fears must indeed be attacked at their source, otherwise unmasking fear is only dodging the issue. By major fear I mean a fear big enough to have originally caused the breakdown and to be now interfering with recovery. I have reserved consideration of such a sufferer for another chapter and have been concerned here only with the person with minor fears whose main problem is no more than how to escape from the physical sensations of fear itself.

> **Fainting** Very few nervously ill people faint. From time to time, many 'feel faint', but few actually faint. This is because the faintness a nervously ill person experiences is so often self-induced and most sufferers, when they start to work themselves up for fear they will faint, usually manage to divert their attention from the fainting to finding an escape route. They are so used to defeating their feeling of faintness by flight, they always sit near a door, so that they can depart quickly if necessary.
>
> But why do they feel faint in the first place? I'm not talking about the person who has been only

'picking at' his food and is possibly undernourished, anaemic. I speak of a nervously ill but adequately fed person. Such a person feels faint because he, in any feared situation, continuously gives himself little shocks by suggesting, 'What if I have to sit near the front? . . . How much longer will I be able to sit through this? . . . Will that man *never* stop talking? . . . What if I do faint? . . . I can feel it coming! . . . What if I can't get out, and faint?' Shock after shock. Most people's nerves can stand this onslaught for a long time and the victim may feel only light-headed. As I said, the nervously ill person rarely faints.

The lesson to be learned is that no nervously ill person need faint if he, or she, is prepared to do as I'm constantly advising – and that is, to not add second-fear. If you are in the situation where you fear fainting, let your body go loose (relax) to the best of your ability and be prepared to accept whatever feelings it brings without adding the extra shock of 'Oh, my goodness, what's going to happen now!'

Some people do faint more readily than others, whether they are nervously ill or not; for example, soldiers on parade, who stand for hours in the same place. This kind of faintness can be corrected by moving one's body as much as the situation permits.

Please don't think, after reading this, that if you have to stand still anywhere that you must immediately begin to fidget. As it is, no nervously ill

person need faint because of his 'nerves' if he lets his
body loosen and accepts whatever feelings it brings
him, even the sensation of 'feeling faint'.

Sedation

If you need sedatives, even in small doses, you must let your
doctor prescribe and supervise the dosage. Do not use other
people's prescriptions. You need not fear addiction from
supervised sedation. When you are well you will not need
sedatives.

Sedation is particularly necessary if you cannot sleep,
because sleep is such an excellent healer. However, sleep is of
most value when it is accompanied by peace of mind. If you
have accepted the strange feelings and are no longer running
away from them, you will have found some peace. Sleep will
now be a boon. But sleep is less helpful to the person who
stays afraid and keeps mentally running away. However,
even here sleep has some restorative power and we rely on
this when we advise sedation.

PALPITATIONS

This short attack of alarmingly quickly beating heart may
come, and so often does, just as you are going off to sleep, or
may even wake you from sleep. Do not sit up in panic. The
more you panic, the more adrenalin is released by your nerves
and the quicker your heart beats. Although you may think,
'Ah, I wish the doctor could feel my pulse now! My heart is
really racing!' I still suspect that if you take your own pulse

you will find that its rate is not much more than one hundred and twenty beats to each minute. Even if it is, it is not important. A healthy heart can tolerate a rate of over two hundred beats per minute for many hours, even days, without evidence of damage – though this is not ideal!

Also, although you may think you can feel your heart beating in your throat and are sure it will burst at any moment, I can assure you it will not. The full bursting feeling is no more than the unusually hard pumping of the main arteries of your neck. Your heart is nowhere near your throat. If you could see how thick and appreciate how powerful your heart muscle is, you would lose all fear of its bursting or being damaged by the palpitations.

So, relax to the best of your ability (see 'How to relax', Chapter 24), take deep breaths, breathing out slowly, and let your heart race until it chooses to slow down, remembering that it is a good heart, merely temporarily over-stimulated, and that such stimulation will not harm it and will soon cease. Should the attack be prolonged does it matter so much? When you understand the palpitations are they so terrible? If necessary you can ease yourself by talking to someone or getting up and drinking a glass of milk. Walking about will not harm your heart even though it is palpitating. If you prefer to stay in bed, by all means do so, but lie there as relaxed as possible and let your heart race *without shrinking from it*. If you do this, one of these nights you will surprise yourself by dropping off to sleep in the middle of an attack.

As acceptance calms your nerves the attacks will be less frequent, until they no longer come. Many years ago when studying under strain, I occasionally had palpitations. I have not had an attack since. Can you see how foolish it would have been had I become agitated by them? My heart served me well during the ensuing years.

SLOWLY BEATING HEART

It may be that instead of beating too quickly, your heart occasionally beats too slowly for comfort and you have attacks of faintness, when you are sure it is about to stop altogether. In such an attack you may feel paralysed, unable to move. This is called a vasovagal attack and is brought on by over-stimulation of the parasympathetic nerve, the vagus. You will remember that the parasympathetic nerves hold the adrenalin-releasing nerves in check. In these attacks they check too severely, and the heart slows to an uncomfortable rate.

Vasovagal attacks are rarer than palpitations, but they are just as disturbing if you do not understand them. Remember, the attack is also the result of *too much nervous stimulation. Your heart is not diseased. The attack does not harm your heart.* As you worry less, sustained tension lessens and the attacks gradually leave you. Even after apparent recovery, you may occasionally have one. Do not be disconcerted by this. With understanding and acceptance they seem less formidable. Actually, your doctor can prescribe tablets to control them, so consult her or him if necessary. It is well to terminate an attack quickly, as it can be exhausting, although not actually harmful. Although I teach facing and accepting, I do not advocate stoical forbearance.

'MISSED' HEARTBEATS

A nervously tired heart, a heart stimulated by too much alcohol, nicotine or caffeine, will sometimes 'miss' beats, although no beat is actually missed. The heartbeats are merely spaced unevenly. The patient feels as if their heart turns over and a tickling sensation catches them in the throat. They may cough and stand still, wondering what will happen next.

'Missed' beats are in no way dangerous and your heart will not stop because of them. They are annoying, but that is all. Exercise abolishes them. So do not let 'missed' beats frighten you into lying on the couch again. Most people over forty have 'missed' beats now and then. Many young people have them. They are not important.

TREMBLING TURNS

Some people have weak turns that are neither palpitations nor attacks of slowly beating heart. They refer to them as 'trembling turns' and describe how their legs suddenly feel weak and tremble and their body breaks out into a clammy sweat. They do not actually faint, although they may feel they will. The attack gradually passes on resting. These are called hypoglycaemic attacks and that long word means merely 'not enough sugar in the blood'. In other words, the engine is knocking for lack of petrol.

Hypoglycaemic attacks come especially to tense people who use their supply of energy faster than they can replenish it. The attack usually occurs before meals and is quite harmless. Resting alone will end it, as the liver then releases sugar into the bloodstream. Eating something sweet helps the attack to pass quickly. It is a good idea to keep some sweets handy. These attacks are not restricted to people with breakdown. Many energetic, healthy people have them.

INABILITY TO TAKE A DEEP BREATH

Just as tension causes scalp muscles to spasm and pain, so does it cause chest and lung muscles to spasm and the patient to complain that she cannot expand her chest sufficiently to take in a deep breath. She may walk round the house sighing until asked by an exasperated relative to 'Please stop those lamentations.'

The effect of such spasm is temporary and is released with relief from tension. It does not harm your chest. Your chest is not diseased. You will always get enough breath, although sometimes perhaps not as freely as you would like.

This shallow breathing can be aggravated by over-breathing in an effort to compensate and get more air into the lungs. Rapid over-breathing washes too much carbon dioxide from the lungs, so that the patient may suddenly feel giddy and her hands, charged with 'pins and needles', may spasm into a tetanic contraction. (The fingers stiffen and the hand flexes at the wrist.) All this is alarming to the patient and her family, but it means so little that breathing into a paper bag and rebreathing the same expired air, although an undignified finish to a spectacular performance, ends it.

'LUMP IN THE THROAT'

Some nervous people complain that they feel a constant pressure in the throat or that they have a 'lump stuck in the throat', which they keep trying to dislodge by swallowing. Some say that their throat seems 'swollen inside'. These patients are convinced that there is something seriously wrong with them, even cancer. Once again we are merely concerned with muscular spasm of nervous origin. We call this *globus hystericus*, which means the hysterical lump. It too will vanish with relaxation and acceptance, although in the meantime it can be so aggravating that the person afflicted finds it difficult to believe that such a definite feeling of pressure can be only spasm. It is not always easy to convince him of the nervous origin of his 'lump' and he is reassured only after the doctor has made a thorough examination of his throat.

GIDDINESS

Giddiness can be a most upsetting phenomenon. To us, the stability of our world depends very much on seeing it as we are accustomed. To suddenly have the impression that the furniture is speeding across the room can indeed be an alarming experience.

Giddiness is of two main types. In one, objects we know to be stationary may seem to move; in the other, we may simply feel unsteady, light-headed. Our balance is normally maintained by such complex co-ordination between eyes, ears and eye and neck muscles, that the slightest deviation from normal may make us sway and feel giddy. So you will appreciate that giddiness may be an early visitor to a fatigued nervous system, although an unimportant one, since it comes only in brief attacks and vanishes quickly with regained composure and loss of fatigue.

As certain small physical defects can cause giddiness, such as a piece of wax stuck to an ear-drum or a blocked eustachian tube (the tube that passes from the ear to the throat), it is as well to have your doctor's assurance that your giddiness is due to 'nerves'. Nervous giddiness is usually the light-headed type.

NAUSEA AND VOMITING

Eating may be a problem. You have probably lost weight and feel nauseated at the sight of food. You may have attacks of vomiting. A gentian mixture before meals may help, but best help of all is a quiet determination to get the food down and keep it there, come what may. If you bring it up, wait a while, take another helping and try again. Accept even this.

Do not make the mistake of thinking that because you feel nauseated and are under stress, your food is doing you little good and that therefore you need not eat much. As long as you swallow the food it will nourish you, although it may take longer than normal to digest. Malnutrition and anaemia can bring symptoms like yours, *so you must eat enough*.

If you have eaten poorly for weeks, your stomach may be unable at first to hold a normal-sized meal. If so, take small meals frequently. Drink egg-flips and plenty of low-fat milk. Also, take a daily dose of vitamins, but only the amount prescribed by a doctor. Too many vitamins can be as dangerous as too few.

So then, however nauseated you feel, be determined to get the food down. This may take time, but you can do it.

LOSING WEIGHT: KEEP OFF THOSE SCALES

Provided you are practising accepting and letting time pass and are eating your meals, especially that last extra bit you don't want, *your weight is not important.* People with nervous breakdown place unnecessary significance on losing weight. They view their protruding bones with growing alarm, wondering just how far the fading-away process can go before they fall to pieces completely. They haunt the bathroom scales, eyes glued to the dial, while they try to jiggle out a few extra grams. *Cover your scales and resist all temptation to stand on them until you are so fat that you think it is time to diet.*

It is interesting to note the direct and yet temporary effect of emotional stress on appetite. I have seen a distressed person heave at the sight of food only to devour it ravenously an hour later after hearing good news.

The body made thin by fear is not diseased and is waiting to recover lost weight as soon as you will pass the food down to it. So place no importance on your wasted looks, your 'poor thin body'. *Eat up and forget those scales.* Even when some cheerful friend says, 'Good heavens, you are thinner than ever!' still resist the temptation to step onto the scales.

No permanent damage

Indeed, when your neighbour gives you a pitying glance and says, 'You look awful!' remember that however ill you may appear today, in a few weeks the same neighbour could be saying, 'You do look different!' You can recover completely from your nervous breakdown. You will not be left with a damaged heart, in spite of the pains you may now feel in that region.

So why not think, 'I may look awful today, but nervous breakdown is not a disease. As soon as I am a little better, I will put on more weight. In the meantime I'll eat up, even if I have to push the food down, and I'll float past my neighbour's comments.'

NO NEW SYMPTOMS CAN ARISE

It may comfort you to know that the action of adrenalin is always restricted to the same organs and so must always follow the same pattern. *There are no more surprises in store for you.* This thought comforts most people because apprehension of what can happen next is a big part of their breakdown. *Other than the symptoms already described, no new symptoms of any significance can arise.*

If you have had only some of the symptoms mentioned do not immediately think you must now experience all the others. It is unusual to have all the symptoms. Each of us has some parts of their body more sensitive than the rest, and which therefore react more readily to stimulation by adrenalin. If you have not been nauseated or have not vomited, it is because your stomach is strong enough to withstand tension. It should continue to do so. We all know that certain people have a tendency to 'heave' when upset, others to run to the toilet, while others just churn inwardly. Few do all three.

Your particular pattern has probably declared itself by now, so you can be comforted by the thought that you have experienced the worst.

17. Being yourself again

Having faced and accepted the disturbing sensations of breakdown, your next question will be, 'How long before I am myself again?' Now, it is almost certain that, despite your new approach to your illness, your symptoms will continue to return for some time – perhaps, at first, as acutely as before you read this book. You will understand this when you appreciate that your adrenalin-releasing nerves will continue to be fatigued and sensitised for a few weeks longer, in spite of the new approach.

I often find that after talking for the first time to a patient with nervous breakdown, she leaves the consulting-room elated and convinced she is cured, sure that she has found the magic wand at last, only to return a few days later disappointed and depressed, in spite of a warning that this could happen. I explain again that her nerves need more time to respond to the new approach; that she is like a runner in a race who, having touched the goal and won the race, must continue to run some yards before she can stop. When these people finally understand and accept this, they take heart.

Understanding and willingness to let more time pass finally work the miracle.

Calm acceptance, *despite delayed recovery*, is your goal. However, although you understand and try to accept calmly, at first you may find calm acceptance very difficult. Do not be disappointed. In the beginning it is enough to direct your thoughts toward acceptance. Calm acceptance will follow in time.

Also, it may be that although you wish to be unafraid, you may still feel fear. Do not be discouraged even by this. *If you can but understand what I have been teaching you, you have made the first step toward recovery.* It is enough at this stage to wish to be unafraid. Provided you make up your mind to accept the strange feelings *although still afraid of them* you will gradually lose your fear, because the decision to accept releases a certain tension and so reduces the intensity of your symptoms. This brings a little hope and you begin to gain confidence in recovery. Complete loss of fear eventually follows.

Do not think I expect you to do this without the help of drug therapy. The right medication can act as a shock-absorber to your nerves and may be prescribed by your doctor. But it is necessary to find the dose that helps to stabilise without a flattening effect. You must have a doctor's help in choosing the type and dose of medicine.

KEEP OCCUPIED

It is essential that you be occupied while awaiting cure. However, I must warn you against feverishly seeking occupation in order to forget yourself. This is running away from fear and you can't run far from fear. I want you to be occupied while facing your symptoms and to accept the possibility of their return from time to time during recovery. There is a world of difference between these two approaches. It is as if you halt your feverish rushing, relax and walk more calmly, thinking to yourself, 'All right! Let the feelings come. Running away won't prevent them. But if I accept them, they will gradually calm down. In the meantime, I'll keep my mind occupied with work, so that I need not think of them unnecessarily.'

Every short respite from fear helps to calm your nerves so that they become less and less responsive to stimulation and your sensations less and less intense, until they are only a memory.

QUICK RECOVERY

I once wrote to a friend in a sanatorium advising her how to recover from her nervous breakdown. Some months later, a stranger telephoned to thank me for the letter, which my friend had shown her. This woman said she knew she was cured before she finished reading it and had been able to leave hospital within a few days. She said that now, four months later, she was still cured and was confident she would never relapse.

Such quick recovery is possible, and when I say you may continue to feel fear and the persistence of symptoms for some time and must be prepared to let more time pass, do not misunderstand and think that I mean that all recovery from breakdown is a long-drawn-out process. Recovery can be, as just illustrated, dramatically quick. I have merely warned you that your recovery may not be as rapid as you expect, so that you will not be unnecessarily disappointed. 'Letting more time pass' means no more than being patient a little longer, but I purposely have not asked directly for patience because the thought of being patient may seem an impossibility to a sufferer from highly tensed nerves. For this reason I chose the phrase 'let more time pass'. The difference is subtle but important. Where the sufferer is prepared to let more time pass, they may think they could not take advice to be patient. The very sound of the word is exasperating.

> **How short is a short illness?** If a sufferer has had no satisfactory treatment for nervous illness, I would call one year of illness short. Illness for a few months would be very short. If a sufferer is having adequate treatment then, in my opinion, three months would be the average time for recovery. I have had patients recover after one interview. Although rare, this has happened.

GRADUAL RECOVERY

Physical exhaustion may delay recovery but, even here, with good food and peace of mind, two or three months are usually long enough to reclaim a person from a nervous breakdown of some severity, provided they do not have too many setbacks. Each patient recovers at their own pace and this depends on the rate of returning confidence and peace of mind. *The strength in a limb may depend on the confidence with which it is used.* When you appreciate that wrong thinking can paralyse some people and keep them bedridden, you will understand how hesitant, diffident thinking can encourage weakness. Returning confidence and physical strength go hand in hand.

Mrs L. had been attending a gymnasium weekly for three years where instructors, interested in the treatment of functional nervous disorders, were so anxious that their clients should not overtax their physical strength, and so insistent that recovery must be gradual that this woman, after three years, had little confidence in her own strength and was prepared to wait even longer for it to return fully.

After I had pointed out that her real trouble was lack of confidence and not muscular weakness and explained that she must free herself from thought-paralysis and use her muscles to strengthen them, she surprised herself by the amount she could do in a few days. She said, 'I'm amazed. I only thought I couldn't do these things. It doesn't seem possible that wrong thinking could have kept me so weak, but it has!' I had a card from her recently and she said, 'I'm still using the golden key you gave me and nobody can see my heels for dust!'

So:

- Do not watch the calendar and time your recovery.
- Let time pass, as little or as much as necessary.
- Let the pace of your recovery look after itself.

- Be concerned only with loss of fear and the use of your muscles.

The mind goes blank, even when feeling much better

Even when feeling better a mind can still suddenly seem to go blank. People like this complain that they can't remember the way they're supposed to be going, although they end by going the right way. They say that they feel as if they are in a dream, even when accompanied.

This is only the shadow of introspection – the result of living so much within themselves. It's not important; never be impressed by it. Wait and it will always pass. Of course, it passes more quickly if you don't add second-fear.

NEVER COMPLETELY OVERWHELMED AGAIN

Sometimes, perhaps when you think you are cured, the old fears and strange feelings may sweep over you again, just as intensely as at the beginning. Don't be dismayed. It is not so strange that they should. Memory is vivid and the scars fresh. Also, you may have gone in search of these sensations to try yourself out, thinking it too good to be true that you are free of the wretched things. Go ahead. You can come to no harm. What has cured you in the past will continue to do so, in spite of any setbacks. So accept each setback quietly and let more time pass.

When you have unmasked the bogey of 'nerves' they can never completely frighten you again. There will always be that inner core of confidence and strength to help you to float past fear. And because this confidence has been born from your own experience you will never quite lose it. You may falter but YOU WILL NEVER BE COMPLETELY OVERWHELMED AGAIN.

And as you lose your fear and regain confidence, you will lose interest in your sensations. You begin to forget yourself for moments and then for hours at a time. Outside interests claim you. You rejoin the world of other people. You are yourself again.

THE PATTERN OF RECOVERY

You recover then by facing, accepting, floating and letting time pass. You are beginning to know this pattern by heart? I hope so, because I want you to know it so well that you make it part of yourself. I want you to understand it so thoroughly that your thoughts fly to it when in doubt or difficulty. It will never fail you, if you apply it correctly.

18. The more complicated nervous illness

Those suffering from the type of breakdown described in the previous chapters had no major problem worrying them other than finding an escape from the physical sensations caused by oversensitised nerves. However, there are many people whose breakdown is caused by apparently insoluble problems, deep sorrow, harrowing guilt or disgrace. The physical sensations of breakdown are only part of their illness and the sufferer is often so engrossed with the cause of breakdown that they pay these physical sensations scant notice until they are well established. Such a breakdown is more complicated than the simpler anxiety neurosis although the two types have much in common and it may sometimes be impossible to draw a sharp line between them.

An apparently insoluble problem with the conflicts it may bring is the commonest cause of complicated nervous breakdown. A problem serious enough to start a breakdown will make the sufferer recoil when he thinks about it. Sometimes the very fineness of his sensibilities, his very regard for honour or his feeling of obligation and duty prevent him making a compromise that another less scrupulous person would make. Most of us with a distressing problem shrink from it at first, but we eventually solve it or compromise, if necessary. The person in danger of breakdown dwells more and more in the unbearable aspects of the problem and finds no solution.

Whatever the problem, if it is grave enough to cause breakdown it will alarm the sufferer so that from time to time, when he thinks of it, he panics. After a while he begins to feel the physical strain of continuous fear and tension and his hands sweat, he feels nauseated, his heart pounds. At first these feelings come mainly when he thinks of his problem or of anything related to it, so that the problem gradually becomes intolerable, accompanied as it is by such upsetting physical feelings.

His day becomes coloured by his 'tragedy'. He may forget it for a few moments and be happy, only to remember it suddenly in the midst of happiness, and his heart sinks like lead. He feels like a drowning man who, every time he comes up for air, is sucked under water again. He may continue for weeks, even months, like this, trying to work but gradually losing all joy in living. Eventually his work suffers. His appearance suffers and his fellow workers notice his strangeness.

This process may be gradual. However, he may go downhill quickly, holding his problem before his eyes all day and having one spasm of panic after another. Whether the downhill course be slow or quick, the pattern is much the same. The more this person dwells on his problem, the more fearful it becomes. What is more alarming, his spasms of fear become more and more intense and the slightest stimulus can start one.

The sufferer becomes bewildered. He cannot understand what has happened and his bewilderment is increased by his vulnerability to suffering. Anything, perhaps something only remotely related to his problem, can make him panic, so he is afraid even to glance at a newspaper.

EXAGGERATED REACTION TO STRESS

Not only is he vulnerable to the fears that his problem inspires, but his reaction to any stress becomes more and more exaggerated, adding to his bewilderment. The stress of waiting is unendurable. It seems as if his brain will snap. The stress of worry becomes a real pain in his head, more than just a headache. It is a searing, pressing, hard pain which nothing seems to relieve. If obliged to do something he dislikes he may be swept by such a storm of painful emotional protest that he stands paralysed before it. And how vulnerable he is to other people's suffering! A sight that we would think merely sad, to him seems tragic. Ordinary events become charged with unnerving poignancy. Most of us are more easily upset when tired: if we magnify this many times, we get a glimmering of the suffering experienced in such a breakdown and can appreciate how bewildering this can be.

This person also becomes sensitised to his imagined unworthiness, and any guilt tucked away in his subconscious is now sure to raise its ugly head. We all have some guilt rationalised into quiescence. The person with nervous breakdown has little hope of keeping guilt rationalised or submerged. As fast as one bogey raises its head and is vanquished, another comes along.

Such a patient brings a long list of guilty suffering which the doctor does his or her best to assuage, only to find a completely new list appearing at the next visit. Guilt can be hell indeed to a person with an oversensitised conscience. The guilt is rarely as great as the sufferer imagines. He has lost his ability to keep it in proportion, because his emotional reactions at the memory of it are so grossly exaggerated. His life to him may seem all guilt.

EXHAUSTION

As time passes the sufferer begins to tire. Nothing is more exhausting than continued emotional stress. At first he could survive much cogitation, even months of it, but gradually his mind and his emotions become fatigued. He has been thinking almost every minute of the day and may be having nightmares as well.

Normally we do not think continually. We may believe that we do, but we do not. Much of the time our brain acts like a receiving set, recording sounds and sights without actually thinking about them. It is in these moments that it rests.

Punishing themselves Some nervously ill people complain that they 'seem to like punishing' themselves. One added, 'That is what nervous illness is all about, isn't it, doctor?'

I have not yet met the nervously ill person who genuinely and deliberately adds to his illness simply to punish himself. His suffering may seem to be self-inflicted because, in his sensitised state, his thoughts, so often fearful, are followed so quickly by distressing symptoms that self-infliction seems the obvious interpretation. Indeed, some therapists believe this, even finding fantastic reasons for it, and they encourage their patients to do the same.

Self-punishment is only apparent; not real. When a nervously ill person says he seems to like punishing himself, he really means, 'Judging from my severe and swift reactions to my vaguest anxious thought, it seems as if I'm purposely punishing myself! I can think of no other explanation!' If such a person really liked punishing himself, he wouldn't be asking for help to stop it.

PLAYING THE RECORD

The person with the absorbing problem thinks about it more and more, until every waking moment is spent in thought and his mind rests only when asleep – and then only if peacefully asleep, which is rarely. Such continuous preoccupation with a small group of ideas has been likened to playing the same record ceaselessly. In the beginning the sufferer can work with the record playing in the background. But gradually it comes between him and his work, between him and his reading, between him and making contact with other people. It takes control of his mind. It becomes his mind. He used to be able to say, 'I won't think of that for a while,' and dismiss the unwanted subject with some success. Now, however hard he tries to get this thing off his mind, he cannot. The harder he fights the more it clings. In other words, *his tired mind has lost its resilience and thoughts race on automatically.*

THE GROOVE

This ceaseless thinking is exhausting, terrifying and bewildering enough, but a new and more alarming phenomenon arises. At least when this person used to think about his problem he could consider it from different points of view, but now, suddenly, he may find that he can see it only from the aspect that has been upsetting him during the past months. He can no longer think 'around' his problem, only 'of' it.

It is as if this viewpoint has worn a deep groove in his mind and his troubled thoughts are automatically channelled into it whenever he thinks of the problem. To see it from another angle seems beyond his power. As soon as he tries to think differently the old distressing picture flashes before him with such vividness and is accompanied by such intense, fearful emotion, that it dismisses all other thoughts. This emotional reaction is triggered so quickly that it is almost a reflex.

Now he becomes truly alarmed. He is convinced he is going mad. It must be a frightening experience to stand helpless before one's own thoughts. One patient said her mind felt like a cork bobbing up and down in a stream, at the mercy of every passing current.

I have mentioned the pain that descends like a tight band around the head and becomes worse with contemplation of the problem. This pain makes thinking so difficult that thought may become confused and slow.

Let me illustrate this type of breakdown by describing the illness of a middle-aged man who came for help. His doctor, in the course of a general examination, had found his blood pressure raised and had said, 'You will probably die with a stroke.' This was the patient's description of the conversation. The stunned man, not wishing to show too much concern, asked few questions but brooded all the way home. Instead of confiding in his wife, he continued to brood and say nothing. This man was about to undertake an important work demanding some years of dedication. Now, without warning, it hardly seemed worthwhile. He became lost in a sad dilemma. What was the use of starting a project with a stroke waiting for him? And yet he was already committed. He became so strained and worried that gradually, whenever he thought of dying with a stroke, the upsetting sensations mentioned above descended upon him.

When he first came to me he was in a pitiful state. I asked his doctor if he could help us both by describing just what was said at that interview. The doctor was surprised at the outcome of his words. Yes, he had mentioned a stroke, but had meant only that in years to come, when this man's time had come to die, he would probably have a stroke. The doctor found it hard to believe that the patient could so easily have misunderstood him and been so unnecessarily upset. He kept saying, 'But he was such a sensible fellow!' So are we all sensible when concerned with somebody else's health and troubles. It is different when it is our own and we are told bad news in a way that shocks us, and leads to misunderstanding.

I explained this to the patient and thought he would get quick relief. Far from it. He came back and said, 'Doctor, you will probably think I am a coward and a fool. I understand all you say, but I can't get it in here.' He tapped his forehead. He continued, 'It is as if my mind is frozen on the subject of stroke. I feel that if something would only crack inside my head, I would get relief and be able to think the way I want to. As it is, I'm not in the race. I automatically feel horror every time I think of a stroke and I can't stop thinking about it. I have only to read something remotely connected with blood pressure to have these reactions.'

He was too exhausted to rise above the conditioned exaggerated expression of his emotional and mental fatigue.

Fear of dying Let me tell you about one old man. He needed an operation on his throat. The surgeon explained that if he had the operation his life could be prolonged by as much as three or four years. The man asked, 'How long will I live if I don't have the operation?'

The surgeon replied, 'About six months.'

'Then,' said the patient, 'I'll settle for six months, thank you. If I go into hospital I'll lose my lodgings and they're very hard to find these days!'

I remember looking at the man in amazement. The surgeon, elderly himself, showed no surprise. He turned and said to us – his group of students – 'The philosophy of old age!' Understanding this was beyond me. Today, I understand it well.

Youth and middle age are for active living and we should not rob it of any of its joy by dreading something that, when it comes, we may actually welcome, or at least, may be unaware of its approach.

Therefore, however old you may be, live each day as it comes and always plan for the future. If, when you are ninety, you need a new tea set, buy it. Don't think, 'I won't buy that. It's too late!' If you have only a little time to enjoy it, enjoy it with what time you have, and enjoy it right up to the very last minute. The days that come when you aren't there won't worry you, because you won't be there to be worried!

Concern yourself only with the days you are alive and enjoy them to their full. Leave the rest to Nature, or to God, as you prefer, and never be bluffed into fearing death, however you imagine it may come.

LOSS OF CONFIDENCE

At this stage in breakdown the sufferer loses all confidence. A little child could lead him. The past months have been spent in 'unending hesitation between two paths', so that now decision, even about small things, requires a Herculean effort which he finds impossible to sustain for longer than a few moments. To decide whether to take an umbrella can be a major problem, almost beyond his power. The umbrella will have a most exciting time, down the path one minute, back in the house the next and then off down the path again. If only rain would come and clinch the matter!

And yet this man is constantly trying to prove that he is still master of himself and not the coward he is beginning to suspect he might be. He is constantly setting fresh tests of endurance and feels more and more obliged to show himself that he can still do 'this' or 'that'. 'I will do it,' he says. 'This is not going to get the better of me.' He does it, but at what expense of nervous energy! Hence, his efforts are short-lived and, as such, often criticised by his friends. In his oversensitised state he thinks his friends are criticising more than they are.

TRICKS OF VISION

In addition he may complain that his sight is affected, that objects appear blurred and thrown into shadow. To remedy this he may keep blinking and screwing up his eyes. Certain objects may appear covered with a shimmering haze like that seen on a hot bitumen road in summer; or they may move spasmodically when viewed from the corner of the eye. Bright light may irritate and he may seek the relief of dark glasses. His everyday glasses need constant readjustment and it is difficult to find a satisfactory pair. This is not surprising since his vision, related as it is to nervous tension, may vary with each examination.

NOISE

Auditory nerves, oversensitised by fatigue, play similar tricks. The gentle contact between spoon and saucer may sound loud enough to make him wince, and television in the house may nearly drive him crazy. Even if he can tolerate the noise, his tired brain has difficulty holding the thread of a plot for more than a few seconds, and most of the time he has withdrawn so much into himself that he cannot follow the dialogue. It is as if the actor moves his mouth but emits no sound. An unnerving sight, to say the least of it, so he retires from the family circle and withdraws even more within himself.

The inability to understand what is happening may now be more alarming than the original conflict or problem, which may have solved itself. The sufferer will walk round the block, head down, thoughts turned inwards, searching for a way out of his nightmare. No solution is permanent, none suits him for long.

It may be just at this stage that life presents extra burdens, domestic trouble, financial worry or perhaps only minor aggravating experiences, trivial enough, but exasperating to him.

For example, a patient was taken to the country for a holiday. On arrival, hanging on the wall at the foot of his bed he found a print of the picture of Van Gogh with his ear cut off. Unfortunately he knew Van Gogh had mutilated himself in this way during one of his mad spells. Just to be in the same room with the picture was almost unendurable strain, yet how could he tell his host he wanted the wretched thing removed? How could he tell him he was terrified of going mad himself and couldn't bear to be reminded of it every time he went into the bedroom? This was a special holiday to help his nerves. Without the Van Gogh he would have had a chance but, of course, it had to be there.

A woman patient went to the seaside for a few weeks. The first day at the beach she noticed a group of women standing at the water's edge looking aimlessly out to sea. They were there the next day and the next. They had such a strange out-of-this-world look about them that she finally asked who they were, only to be told they were the inmates of a city mental institution down on holiday. Of all times in the year they had to choose this! Those women seemed to dog her footsteps in that small village and she said she never failed to see the shadowy form of herself trooping along at their rear.

THE EXHAUSTED FAMILY

There is the added anxiety of watching the family, one by one, become tired and exasperated. They are feeling the strain of alternately hoping and despairing. One of them is bound to say something further to upset the patient. One woman, who went to her husband saying she thought she was going mad, was told, 'Well, there are plenty of places to send people who go like that.' He was the kindest of husbands, but his nerves were so tensed by the continuous strain of trying to help and placate his wife and not say the 'wrong thing', that he scarcely knew what he was saying. As it was he could hardly have done more harm had he taken the last straw and placed it on her back himself.

DEPRESSION

Depression is born from emotional fatigue. If depression strikes suddenly as a strong physical feeling, it can be a shattering experience and it is hard to believe that the world is still a good place to live in and that recovery is worthwhile and possible. The sufferer rarely understands that this is but another expression of his extreme exhaustion. Our moods are so much part of us that it is difficult to regard them dispassionately. When the world seems black it is not easy to say, 'It is I who is out of sorts, not the world.'

The fight becomes grimmer and grimmer as depression and apathy rob their victim of the desire to recover. Every moment becomes a torture; even to comb her hair is an unendurable physical and spiritual effort, so she may begin to look unkempt.

AGITATION

This person is now fatigued almost beyond human endurance and yet she cannot rest. Exhausted nerves become agitated nerves, so she feels impelled to rush about, although she can hardly drag her tired body along. How she longs to rest, yet when she does all the devils of torture plague her. What can she do? Where can she go? Her mood swings from depression to hysterical reaction. At times she may find relief in tears.

It is at this stage that obsession may begin.

OBSESSION

Obsession is one of the most alarming manifestations of nervous breakdown and more than any other symptom convinces the sufferer that she must be on the way to madness. And yet it can start so simply in a fatigued person. Most of us have a mild obsession or two; for instance, the woman who, on going out, must return and check the taps or gas-jets although she knows perfectly well she turned them all off before leaving.

Obsession that comes with nervous breakdown is more demanding than this and is characterised by repeated compulsive thought or action which is always distasteful, even fearful, to its victim. For example, the patient afraid of having a stroke developed the most aggravating obsession. When he stooped, the blood rushing to his face reminded him so forcibly of his blood pressure and the stroke to come that he invariably thought, 'Stroke!' The harder he tried not to do so, the more surely he did. Sometimes he even said the word aloud. When new power switches were put into his home, he ordered them to be placed waist-high so that he need not stoop.

Then there was the sick nurse who had babies under her care and could not pass a window in the hospital without feeling the urge to throw the baby in her arms into the street below. The list is long and no benefit will be gained by detailing it here. If you have obsessions it is necessary only that you should understand how they have come about and know how to cure them.

Most of us know the difficulty of banishing a tune from our mind when tired. A tired mind loses its resilience and an unwanted tune or thought sticks like a fly to fly-paper. In other words, the obsession of a sufferer with breakdown is caused by no more than unwelcome auto-suggestion which, coming at a time when emotions are so grossly exaggerated, makes such an overpowering impression on other fatigued minds that it becomes firmly established there.

Anyone who has not experienced nervous breakdown may think I have painted an unnecessarily grim picture. I can assure such a reader that no part is worse than the description. My reason for exposing every detail is simple. This book is written mainly for the person with a nervous breakdown or 'bad nerves', and it is a revelation to them to learn that their mysterious and bewildering symptoms are no more than those of breakdown in general and have been experienced by many before them. To them their body has been a Pandora's Box of unpleasant surprises and they have lived in dread of what might appear next. When the whole box of tricks is laid out before them and they understand what they are facing, it loses much of its terror.

You have probably seen yourself in part, if not in all, of this description. It is possible that you have difficulties not mentioned here, but the principle of treatment outlined in the next chapters will meet all those difficulties.

19. How to cure the more complicated nervous illness

Although the nervous breakdown caused by problem, sorrow, guilt or disgrace usually brings a very harassed sufferer to the doctor with complicated symptoms, the same fundamental plan of treatment described for the simpler type of breakdown cures them, namely:

- facing
- accepting
- floating
- letting time pass

Each of the four main causes of breakdown – problem, sorrow, guilt and disgrace and their side-effects such as obsession, sleeplessness, depression, etc. – will be discussed in a separate chapter.

Before studying treatment the four following conditions for cure should be read and a resolution made to obey them.

1. Carry out instructions wholeheartedly. A half-hearted try is useless.

2. Never be completely discouraged by apparent failure. *However severely you may seem to fail on occasions, failure is only as severe as you will let it be. The decision to accept and carry on turns the worst failure into success. There is no 'point of no return' in nervous breakdown.* A day of deep despair can be followed by a day of hope, and *just when you think you are at your worst you can turn the corner to recovery.* Your emotions are so variable in breakdown, try not to be too impressed by your unhappy moods, and *never be completely discouraged.*

3. There must be no self-pity. And this means *no self-pity.* There must be no dramatisation of self in this 'terrible state'. No thinking of how little the family understands, how little they realise how ghastly this suffering is. Self-pity wastes strength and time and frightens away those who would otherwise help you. If you are honest with yourself you will admit that some of your self-pity is pride: pride that you have withstood so much for so long. Of this you can be justly proud, and let recognition of this endurance give you confidence when you approach this new method of treatment. When I mention self-pity to some patients they look at me blankly. It had not occurred to them to pity themselves, so busy were they being bewildered. But others know exactly what I mean.

4. There must be no regretting and sighing 'if only . . . '. What has happened, if it cannot be remedied, is now past, finished. The present and the future must be your main concern. Life lies ahead. So remember, no more 'if onlys'. A man came for help whose sad story was so full of 'if only' that his nails were bitten down almost to the quick. However hard I tried to convince him that he should now cease regretting, accept the past and plan for the future, he continued to return saying, 'Now, if only . . . '. In vain I tried to make him understand that he must find occupation to help himself regain stability. He kept saying he was too exhausted to work and far too preoccupied with his problems. His main problem was desertion by his wife. She had left him and gone to the country. During the time I treated him she came to town and inquired if he were working yet. It is possible that had the answer been 'Yes' she would have returned to him. As it was she went back to the country. The next day he came to me saying, 'Doctor, you remember telling me to get a job? Well, I'm sure that if I'd had one my wife would have come back. Now, if only I'd listened . . . '. He was off again. Surely there is no need to say more to convince you that your path must lie ahead. You will often regret and often think 'If only . . . ' – that is human, but do not let regret hinder recovery.

So:

- Carry out instructions wholeheartedly.
- Never be completely discouraged by failure.
- Have no self-pity.
- Let there be few regrets and fewer 'if onlys'.

20. Problems

If some distressing problem has brought you to a state of advanced emotional and mental exhaustion you have probably realised that you now have small hope of making lasting decisions about your problem without help. You will certainly try to force yourself to do so, at great expense of nervous energy, but you will probably be unable to hold any decision for long and will make new, even momentous decisions, every little while. One moment you will think you have everything straightened out and feel happy about it. And then you find, perhaps only an hour or two later, some new aspects of the problem that send you off into indecision again.

It may be a hardship to think at all. You may be so slowed by fatigue that you grope for thoughts, enveloped by one wave of panic after another. Or your thoughts may have reached the stage where they consistently turn into the same distressing groove, and deliberation over your problem seems impossible. In this condition it is essential that you seek help. You must have someone with whom to discuss your troubles and help you find a satisfactory and stabilised way of looking at them. Only then will your tired mind rest.

IT MAY NOT DEPEND ENTIRELY ON YOU

It is as if you must temporarily use your helper's mind as your own, until your mind recovers from its fatigue. This is an excellent example of how untrue are the well-worn complacent sayings, 'It all depends on you,' and 'Your recovery is in your own hands – it's up to you.' *Your recovery may not rest only in your own hands. You most certainly may need help.* When I explained this to a harassed woman recently she burst into tears and said, 'Please don't take any notice of my tears. I'm so relieved to hear you say I need help. I feel too utterly spent to help myself much and yet everyone insists that it depends entirely on me, that no one can really help me but myself. I have felt so overwhelmed and hopeless at the thought of this, that to hear you say I need help is such relief, it is almost too much to bear!'

Do not feel ashamed or discouraged if you feel you need help. An injured leg may need a crutch, why not a shocked, tired mind? But choose your helper as carefully as you can. Let it be your wisest and not just your nearest friend. You are now so impressionable that the wrong advice could be upsetting and could temporarily hinder recovery. It is a temptation to choose the nearest confidant. You may have noticed how readily you confide in a stranger. As one woman expressed it, 'To my shame, I find myself baring my soul to strangers and I don't seem to be able to do much about it.' Try not to talk to many and so confuse yourself with different opinions. Choose one wise friend and keep to her or him.

If you have no such friend, find a suitable minister, priest or doctor. If you choose a religious confidant, be sure they will not think it their duty to make you more aware of your guilt. You are probably too much aware of this already and too willing to castigate yourself, with dire results. At this stage you need comfort, not chastisement.

ACCEPT THE NEW POINT OF VIEW

After suitable deliberation with a well-chosen adviser you must be prepared to accept, for the time being at least, the solution or compromise you both find. Do not expect a perfect solution. When you are well you can modify it if necessary: it will be far easier to do so then than now. But it is essential that at this stage *you end your ceaseless pondering and are given one point of view to hold in your tired mind*. The solution finally decided upon *must be acceptable to you*. There is nothing more soul-searing than trying to follow blindly a pattern not acceptable to one's heart. So do not persevere with a solution which you feel, deep within yourself, is not the right one. Peace cannot be forced in this way. It is essential that the new view causes a minimum of pain and fear. A wise counsellor will see to this. Ask them first to read this book, so that they will understand the part expected of them.

Talking about the new point of view will help to impress it on your mind. Also, ask your friend to write it down as simply as possible, so that you can refer to it when alone. I repeat, *holding one point of view will act as a crutch for your tired mind*. It delivers you from ceaseless cogitation and its resulting emotional and mental fatigue. You may not find a viewpoint entirely without pain, but knowing it is the best available brings some peace, some respite.

To discuss your problem with another may mean forcing yourself to expose something, the mere thought of which brings on such paroxysms of fear that you may think you are incapable of dragging yourself to your friend. Do not make the mistake of forcing yourself to go, of fighting your way there. You will arrive exhausted if you do. Use the pattern of recovery described earlier and *float there*. Do you remember the woman who could not enter a shop until she learned the trick of floating? Follow her example and imagine you are floating. It works like magic. As I have explained, when you think of floating you subconsciously relax and this lessens the tension which has been inhibiting action. So float to your friend, don't fight your way there. In addition, try to *let all disturbing, obstructive thoughts float away, out of your head*.

THE IRON BAND

It is possible that at this stage the mere thought of talking about, or even thinking of, your problem will cause your scalp muscles to spasm and bring the iron band of pain around your head. Do not be dismayed by this. You can still think, *if you are prepared to accept the pain and relax your head muscles to the best of your ability*. You may be forced to think slowly, and because of this may feel confused. Accept the slow thought and confusion without panic. Do not fight it by tensing your muscles and trying to force thought. If you relax with acceptance you will find that you can still think adequately, however slowly. *There is nothing wrong with your brain, its work is only being hindered by pain, fear and fatigue. Its eventual recovery will be complete.*

OLD FEARS RETURN

While you are discussing your problem with your confidant you may feel overwhelming relief and think you are cured at last. This may be true, especially if you have not had such help before. This person may give you such healing comfort and such a satisfactory solution to your problem that you may have no more suffering. Also, confession alone can cure, if your troubles called for confession.

However, if you have suffered for months and have already experienced discussion and confession, although you may feel immediate relief when you discuss your problems again, the relief may be temporary. Your nerves are still fatigued and so may yet play tricks on you. You may think you have straightened out your problem with your adviser only to find, when you are alone again, that some hitherto unsuspected and undiscussed aspect presents itself, and once more alarming, exaggerated reactions throw you into panic.

Or you may find that, while able to follow your friend's reasoning when with her, and able to hold it for some time after leaving her, your old fears eventually return and you lose your grip on the new point of view. Do not despair at this. It is to be expected. After all, you have been looking at the problem for so long from the one distressing viewpoint that it would be almost a miracle if this did not soon reassert itself vividly. It has become your habit pattern.

So if you find that the old point of view returns with all its upsetting accompaniments, go once more to your friend, tell her about it and discuss your problem again. Indeed, you may have to visit her often before you can grasp and hold firmly the new point of view.

As mentioned, it is a great help if your adviser writes down a few notes for you. I make such notes for my patients and, if necessary, with the patient's consent show a member of their family how to help them. I sometimes coach the very member who has been most unsympathetic and who may have been making the patient's life even more of a burden. In this way I have turned a hindrance into a help. It is surprising how enthusiastic such people can become when they think they have the doctor's confidence and that she is turning to them for co-operation. From being critical of the doctor they uphold her opinion as if it were the final appeal.

GLIMPSING THE NEW POINT OF VIEW

If, after obtaining the help of your friend or perhaps some member of your family, you find that you can hold the new viewpoint for only a few moments each day, do not be discouraged. *If you can just glimpse it for a fleeting moment daily, you will have made a beginning.* Eventually, with practice you will hold it for longer and longer, until you make it the final, established point of view.

Let me illustrate this with a story about a farmer's wife. She had lived happily with her husband and children on a small farm with good friends near by until she became ill with pneumonia. During her convalescence the children were sent to boarding school and the friends moved farther into the country, so that this woman was left lonely and unemployed when she most needed company and occupation. Days spent on the farm became a misery.

Had she realised at this stage that her troubles were the expression of exhaustion following pneumonia, she would have been saved much additional suffering. As it was, she became bewildered and afraid of her condition and, on the advice of a friend, visited a psychoanalyst. She made an unfortunate choice, was inexpertly analysed, and an odd collection of small, pathetic guilt complexes was exposed as it would be in any one of us similarly treated. The analyst made much of this guilt and of course, with his encouragement, so did the patient, so that she now found herself with a bunch of problems to solve. She became more apprehensive and depressed and developed a protracted nervous breakdown.

She could not understand why the home she had loved and where she had been so happy could upset her now, so that she could hardly bear to think about it. She did not wish her husband to be obliged to sell at that time because this would have been financially unwise. She asked, 'I just want to live happily at home, but this seems utterly beyond my power. What has happened to me? I seem to be a different person.' She said that as soon as she drew near the place a wave of such deep revulsion swept over her that she wanted to run away.

I explained to her that she was looking at the situation from two conflicting points of view. First, she saw the farm as a place where she had recently suffered deep depression and the memory was so vivid and frightening that she was convinced that the same suffering, or worse, was waiting to claim her again as soon as she entered the house. Secondly, and at the same time, she saw her home as the place where she had lived happily in the past and where she wanted to do so again.

I explained that she must put before herself the picture of living contentedly there and must be prepared to wait for time to pass until this picture became reality. *It would take time for the memory of her suffering to fade.* Until it did, she could not expect much happiness there. She might have happy moments, but *only time could establish happiness by fading the memory of unhappiness.*

In the meantime she must be occupied and let each day pass *without watching her own reactions and analysing her feelings.* The feelings of the present and the immediate future were sure to be mixed, uncertain and painful, coloured as strongly as they were by the recent past, so why be impressed by them? She must be prepared to live through the next few months while she gradually floated toward her goal. *Wanting to live at home happily was enough foundation to build on.* I explained that by 'float' I meant she must let time carry her to happiness, and must not ask for quick recovery. She must try to let all upsetting memories, or destructive auto-suggestion, float away out of her head.

As it is not wise for depressed people to be alone for long, I advised this woman to make frequent visits into town and to invite a friend to stay with her while waiting for the new point of view to become established. It is inestimable help to a patient with a nervous breakdown just to hear another person moving about the house.

STICK TO THE NEW POINT OF VIEW

If you wish to forget an upsetting point of view do so by finding a more acceptable substitute and when you have found one, *stick to it*. If changed circumstances make readjustment necessary, consult your adviser, unless you are so much better that you are certain you can manage unaided. If you have any doubts about yourself you must seek help again, otherwise you will be caught in the same old habit of thinking one way one moment and another the next.

It is not necessary to make your own decisions at this stage. You gain no lasting benefit by trying to do so. Above all, *do not waste time being upset because you cannot make decisions*. Realise you are like this because of fatigue and that as soon as you are well again you will be as capable as ever of making up your own mind, perhaps after this experience more capable. I emphasise, it is not important that you make decisions now. It is important only that you and your adviser arrive at one decision about your problem and that you abide by it and so rest your tired brain.

A man who complained of being unable to make decisions was told that he had but to make a supreme effort and reach a decision and his battle would be won. From then on, added his adviser, he would have no more trouble making decisions.

This advice was misleading. This person may make a great effort and successfully arrive at one decision, but that will not alter the fact that his mind is still non-resilient and his nervous system exhausted, so that in the immediate future it could be just as difficult as ever for him to make decisions. Why place so much importance on the necessity for a tired mind to make decisions? When the mind rests with relief from fear, decisions will be more easily made.

THE INSOLUBLE PROBLEM

On being advised to find a solution or a compromise to their problem, some people think, 'My problem has no solution, so there's no way out for me.' I have seen too many apparently 'insoluble' problems solved to be impressed by this. Your problem may seem insoluble to you, but you would be surprised at what an experienced counsellor can unravel. If little can be done to alter a situation at least he can teach you to look at it from a less distressing point of view. For example, a woman made ill by living with a mother-in-law of whom it was impossible to be rid, said, 'So, you see, doctor, there is no solution for me.'

I explained that there was no solution while she regarded her mother-in-law's absence as the only way out of the difficulty. I suggested that instead of looking at the elderly woman with hate, she should make a determined effort to concentrate on her good points and see if she could feel differently toward her. People react to our opinion of them, and very often act toward us as they subconsciously think we expect them to. The older woman must have known of her daughter-in-law's dislike, and probably, as a result, unwittingly turned her worst side toward the younger woman. Happily the young woman came to understand this and was successful in changing the situation.

TRUE ORGANIC SICKNESS

It is not easy to be philosophical about ill health based on organic sickness that is not 'just nerves'. If such illness is the cause of your breakdown you need aid from an understanding doctor because, even here, there may be a medical point of view which can help you.

For many years an old friend of mine, now aged eighty-five, has had persistently high blood pressure. Fifteen years ago, when she first knew about the pressure, she was about to succumb to the fear of an imagined imminent stroke. However, after a few quiet talks her doctor was able to help her view the situation sensibly. How fortunate that he did, otherwise this woman could have spent the last fifteen years of her life fearfully awaiting a stroke that did not come.

CHANGE OF SCENE

In nervous breakdown there may be the stultifying repetition of the same old familiar scene and a daily encounter with painful memories associated with it. Many a person craves change and feels that he should not be battling against such odds as these. However, his friends so often advise him to 'stick to his guns' that he stays, thinking that to flee the scene would be considered cowardly.

A situation should be carefully considered before advising anyone to stay on the scene of breakdown. If leaving would be running away from something that should be faced, then I recommend staying. However, even here it is often wise to leave temporarily until more rested. For example, a young schoolteacher came with a breakdown caused by failing to control a class of unruly pupils. I did not advise this woman to quit and find a different school. Had she done so, she may have met another unruly class or at least would have always lived in dread of doing so. I advised her to have a month's holiday and then return and face the class with a new method of approach. She was successful in time and very pleased that she had not changed schools.

But when a man suffering from breakdown because his wife had left him came for help I advised him to leave the home charged with her memory until he had developed some immunity, or, better still, to leave town for six months if possible. Wounds that are opened daily heal too slowly.

So the circumstances of each person must be assessed before recommending complete change of scene. However, short changes are good for all and are often advocated. They act as mild shocks, relieve the fatigue engendered by repetition and so help the sufferer to see himself and his problem in better perspective.

A young man suffering from breakdown visited an unfamiliar seaside resort with friends. On entering the hotel lounge he noticed a cheerful group of people talking by a sunny window and an unusual small carved model of an old sailing-ship suspended from the rafters. That glimpse of interesting difference arrested his racing thoughts, drew him out of himself, and he suddenly had insight into his strange condition. For the first time he realised that he was emotionally spent and that because of this he had his problems completely out of proportion. They were not as insuperable as he had imagined. He saw that were he well he could probably cope with them.

This young man described how, late that same evening, tense and distraught, he waited for his friends to return from a swim. The strain of simply waiting for someone to return so that he could settle for the night was almost intolerable. He felt his brain would snap. This, following on the incident in the lounge, showed him even more clearly that the trouble lay within himself, in his own exhausted physical state, and not in his problems.

Some people in a similarly spent condition complain that they feel as though they are groping beneath a low, flat, dark, unyielding ceiling which seems to press them down whenever they try to rise above their problems and think clearly. Others describe their mind as feeling as if enveloped in a grey blanket from whose folds it cannot free itself. When one remembers that eyesight may also be affected so that landscape may appear thrown into shadow even on a bright day, one can appreciate how easily these people may develop a feeling of withdrawal from the rest of the world.

This grey ceiling, or blanket, is no more than accentuated brain-fatigue. Students experience something of this when, after three or four hours of continuous study, they suddenly feel they cannot pack in another word and must go outside and hose the garden until their mind clears. The person with breakdown has been studying his problem for weeks, months, without hosing his garden. It is not strange that his mind should feel grey, unresponsive, non-resilient and so very, very tired.

It is not unusual to find these people craving to be on top of a high mountain or in an aeroplane where, they imagine, the feeling of looking down on the world below would free them from this imprisoned feeling of being under everything. This person really needs sleep, days and nights of it. Sleep, and the rest that it brings from ceaseless, anxious thinking.

As the sufferer recovers, the curtain lifts from time to time and he has moments of joy when he can think freely and direct his thoughts with his old accustomed agility. The first moment of normal thinking may come almost as a revelation. The young man described above said that a few days after he returned from the seaside a friend asked him to bandage a cut finger. Suddenly, during the 'operation', the curtain lifted and he almost shouted, 'I can think clearly again!'

This man was intelligent and was able to trace the cause of his symptoms and treat himself, asking for little help. He described how, after that experience when bandaging the finger, the curtain soon descended again, to lift a few hours later. During the next few days it would lift one minute and descend the next, so that he could never be sure of himself. It was as if his mind were fragile and he must handle it with care lest it should break. He felt himself growing tense, trying to steady his mind and keep the curtain from descending. Then he remembered my words about floating, and he relaxed and accepted the hovering curtain and waited for more time to pass.

Some friends in a distant state asked him to visit them and he knew that were he to go, the complete and sudden change would be so refreshing that the curtain would lift permanently and he would step right out of breakdown. He preferred to stay and prove to himself that he could recover on his own ground without outside help. When he finally was freed he said it was as if he were reborn. Everything now shone as never before. Colours were brighter, more vivid; the blue of the sky seemed exquisite, and a feeling of such happiness and benevolence toward all things welled up within him that he could not bear to hurt even an ant. He has never completely lost that feeling. If you are suffering as this young man, the same reward awaits you. The law of compensation works particularly well after recovery from nervous breakdown.

This does not mean that you should refuse a change of scene if offered it. You need not prove anything to yourself. You can take this young man's word that it is possible to come out of breakdown on your own ground without going away. But if you have suffered, why prolong it? The opportunity of having a complete change should be grasped and the relief that it can bring, accepted.

So:

- Discuss your problem with a wise counsellor until you find a satisfactory solution or compromise; search for a second picture.
- Stick to the new point of view, and be contented if at first you can only glimpse it each day.
- Remember that having one approach to your problem acts like a splint for a tired mind.
- If fatigue makes concentration difficult, do not tensely try to force thought; be prepared to think as slowly as your tired brain allows.
- Do not despair if old fears return; accept all setbacks and float on to recovery.
- Do not place importance on making your own decisions while ill.
- Accept a change of scene if it is offered.

21. Sorrow

Although overwhelming sorrow can temporarily disorganise our lives, it is not so complicated to manage as apparently insoluble problems. Sorrow may bring problems, it is true, but these are usually overshadowed by the grief itself. Deep sorrow alone can cause breakdown without the addition of conflict or guilt. However, when the source of such breakdown is studied, it is usual to find fear somewhere involved. As mentioned earlier, sorrow at the loss of a loved one is mixed with the fear of facing the future alone.

BROODING

Many of us, when we suffer deeply, may think we are overwhelmed; however, as time passes, life carries us with it and we rally and find happiness. But there are people who become so affected by sorrow, and whose environment offers such little encouragement, that they find it impossible to lead a normal existence. They sit and think only of their ill fate. This continuous melancholic brooding gradually exhausts their emotional reserves, so that their reactions become exaggerated; their sadness becomes deeper and deeper, the waves of despair more and more overwhelming, and the body subjected to this assault becomes less and less able to withstand it.

These people eat and sleep little and literally fade away. Finally the mind becomes so exhausted, it perceives and thinks so slowly, that it seems impossible to communicate with them. They stare vacantly and answer hesitatingly, if at all.

If, however, by some means, the chain of sorrow–brooding–sorrow can be broken, the sufferer is capable of accepting life again.

THE SUFFERING HABIT

So much of our suffering is due to memory and habit. We remember what we suffered yesterday and fail to appreciate the difference between reality and memory. A woman's husband had been dead six months; no grieving could bring him back; she lived in a large farmhouse with a family who needed her care. That was reality, and after intensive in-patient treatment she recognised it. And yet before treatment she spent her time brooding over the memory of the past until nothing but that existed, and that certainly was not reality.

Suffering soon brings fatigue, which brings more fatigue, because we grow so tired of feeling tired. However, let us bring even a little hope into our destructive thinking and we can begin to reverse the process. Hope with its forward projection also becomes memory, but an uplifting one. If we were hopeful yesterday, we can be a little more so today and even more so tomorrow, until all our days bring hope. If we are fortunate, circumstances force concentration on other things. A mother with children to care for usually recovers sooner from the death of her husband than a childless widow.

It is surprising how, even after much sorrow, we can be happy again as time passes. A woman who had had more sorrow than it would seem possible to live with, and who had lost all desire to live, said that one day, when feeling almost completely overwhelmed, she made herself go outside and burn up some garden refuse. By chance she threw some fresh leaves onto the fire. The pungent smell of burning leaves gave her a moment of unexpected pleasure and at the same time a cheeky little bird flashed past and cavorted on a branch beside her. She could not help smiling. This experience was the turning point in her illness. It showed her that she was still capable of feeling pleasure; that such feeling was not quite as dead as she had thought. This gave her enough hope to cling to and she now lives as peacefully and happily as most of us.

AVOID UNNECESSARY SUFFERING

If you find living with your dead husband's armchair upsets you, put it away until you can look at it with less suffering. A friend of mine refused to remove her husband's chair, saying, 'I loved him when alive, why should I now avoid things that remind me of him?' While praiseworthy, this was a waste of emotional effort. For months, every time she passed the chair she suffered. She would sometimes feel moderately cheerful until she saw the chair. In the end she let us remove it, temporarily. Had she done so earlier, she would have been saved unnecessary suffering. It would have been sensible, not cowardly, as she had thought. It is sometimes good to know when to run away from suffering. Our subconscious makes a good burial ground and it is not wise to dig there unnecessarily.

DESERTION

While death causes sorrow, at least there is no great conflict attached to it. It is final and we must accept it. Time will help us now. Sorrow that is being constantly revived, as occurs in desertion by wife or husband, is much harder to bear. The one hears about the other, and salt is repeatedly rubbed into the wound. Injustice may be involved and this is hard to accept. But even here, the years gradually change sorrow into acceptance and forgetfulness. One woman was very close to breakdown after her husband left her. Now, five years later, she would not change the pattern of her life to take him back. And yet, when he went I could never have convinced her that in such a short time she would prefer his absence.

It is well to remember that *none of us depends entirely on another for our happiness*, although we may think we do. It is not the person we love who is responsible for our depth of feeling. This feeling is part of ourselves, is our capacity to love and it stays with us despite misfortune.

So, should the person you love have left you, do not think the end of the world has come. You still have a great capacity for loving and it is possible to love someone else as much, perhaps even more, although you may shrink indignantly from this suggestion today. *Let time pass and do not hesitate to put your faith in the healing power of its passing.*

BEAR NO GRUDGE

If you have been hurt, do not make the mistake of thinking you will find relief by taking revenge or watching retribution catch up with the offender. Do not burn yourself up with the desire to 'get even'. To find lasting peace you must forget vengeance. The Bible gives good advice about this. It is only too true that should retribution find the one who has hurt us, we rarely feel the pleasure we anticipated. We are much more likely to have ceased being interested, or may even feel sorry for the 'poor devil'. So, don't waste time and energy being revengeful now.

When you decide to take the kindest course, it is surprising how complications that may have seemed insuperable have a knack of disappearing. Can you see how much more peaceful and wholesome such a course would be than being burnt up and kept tensed by hatred, bitterness and impatience for revenge?

So:

- Accept your sorrow philosophically.
- Do not sit and brood.
- Occupy your time.
- Be determined to bring hope into the picture.

- Temporarily remove objects that bring painful memories.
- Remember that nobody's happiness depends entirely on another.
- Leave vengeance to God or Nature.

22. Guilt and disgrace

GUILT

Guilt can be a nightmare to some people suffering with nervous breakdown, particularly to those trying to set a high standard for themselves, such as religious people who lead a dedicated life.

Guilty thoughts

The guilt may be associated only with thoughts. Such thoughts assume undue importance to these saintly people, who struggle to banish them by fighting them, by trying not to think them. I explain to these patients that continued recurrence of these thoughts is due to no more than fear and memory working together. As such, they will cling for the time being and must be temporarily accepted. These particular thoughts have been recurring for weeks, months or longer. They are deeply entrenched. Thinking them has become such a habit, what hope would anyone have of banishing them immediately, on command? And yet how desperately some try to do just that. The only chance of obliterating them under these conditions would be to fall unconscious or into a dreamless sleep.

When I point this out the victim usually feels great relief because he realises that, even though the thoughts may hold an element of reluctant enjoyment, he is not such a particularly sinful person after all, just an ordinary human being reacting in a normal way.

Understanding banishes fear for many, and with fear lost the battle is won. The unwelcome thoughts come but they no longer mean so much, so that by degrees, whether they are there or not no longer matters and forgetfulness eventually follows.

Unwanted thoughts Never make the mistake of fighting to be rid of unwanted thoughts; relax toward them, let them come, take them with you – but WILLINGLY – and see even the most shocking for what they are: only thoughts.

If you fight to forget unwanted thoughts, or try to replace them with others, you make the unwanted thoughts too important so that forgetting becomes more and more difficult. It is always difficult to forget on command, especially if mentally tired.

A lot of practice at accepting and working while accompanied by upsetting thoughts may be needed to change them into 'just thoughts' with no upsetting reaction, holding no fear. Without fear, thoughts that once seemed to almost mesmerise can finally come to no longer matter. No-longer-mattering is the goal; *not*

forgetting. One can never be sure of forgetting;
memory is a great hoverer. However, if no-longer-
mattering has been achieved through understanding
and experience, one can depend on it with confidence.

Of course, from time to time, mattering will return.
However, when not-mattering has been felt, if only for
a moment, the mustard seed of confidence this
brings will never actually disappear. As the sufferer
pulls himself out of each setback by rediscovering
not-mattering, it becomes in-built and comes quickly
to his rescue whenever a setback threatens. The prize
has been won.

Guilty action

If some past guilty action is an important part of the cause
of your breakdown, confess and make reparation if possible,
but do not be disappointed if you do not immediately feel
the relief expected. Your nervous system is still fatigued and
will probably find some other guilt in exchange for the old.
Do not be impressed by this. Try to see it for what it is, no
more than *the unbalanced reaction of an exhausted nervous
system.*

While guilt alone can start a nervous breakdown, it is
more usual for a guilt complex to arise in the course of an
already established breakdown. The mind, made sensitive
and non-resilient by fatigue, fastens quickly onto some real
or imagined guilt. So persistent is this feeling that its owner
may find himself grappling with one guilty episode after
another.

So when you have unburdened yourself of your present guilt enjoy the relief you may feel. It may be lasting, but do not be disappointed if it is not. When cured, you will feel your guilt so much less acutely, you will be able to consider it rationally and keep it in proportion.

Guilt that cannot be confessed and forgiven

Religious people can repent in prayer or at confession, so that even if they have harmed someone now dead, they can find solace. If you are in a similar situation, but can find no help in religion, face the facts squarely and decide to make amends in some way. Do not force yourself to do this immediately if the strain seems too great. It is enough to decide now to make amends later. I emphasise this aspect of not forcing because one of the principles of treatment is to give yourself as little extra strain as possible while ill. You and your adviser must judge how important to your recovery are immediate confession and reparation and act accordingly.

We all have countless ancestors whose frailties we are bound to have inherited in some measure. Few of us can reach middle age without some skeleton rattling in our cupboard. In fact, most of us have a fine collection hidden away, but we wisely manage to lose the key. To let past guilt paralyse present action is destructive living. Let us recognise our guilt if it declares itself, make what reparation we can, but with a quiet determination live on, philosophically laying some of the blame at the feet of our ancestors, some at the feet of those who trained or neglected to train us, and some at our own feet. But let us make amends by leading from now on (in your case when you are well) worthwhile, constructive lives.

Another chance

It would soon be an empty world if the guilty ones decided they could not live on because of their guilt. How much more commendable it is to live on cheerfully, accepting the burden of guilt. This in itself is part penance. So, *always give yourself the benefit of another chance. You can never fall so far that you cannot rise again and be a fine person*, if you make up your mind to do so. The farther the fall, the steeper the climb and the greater the effort needed for recovery, admittedly, but the character of the person who finally emerges triumphantly is so much finer for that extra effort.

Such endeavour does not mean gritting your teeth and fighting an uphill battle, constantly reminding yourself of your objective. It simply means putting before you the picture of the person you want to be and letting time carry you to its realisation. This picture will materialise more easily if, each morning before rising, you take the time to think about it. You need make no further conscious effort to remember it during the day. You strengthen your subconscious with a daily reminder which helps to condition your actions until practice establishes the habit you seek. There is no grim battle to fight. Harness your subconscious, direct its powerful machinations with a daily reminder and let it work a miracle for you. It can.

But remember, you must never be completely discouraged by failure. Sometimes you will think you have lost sight of your goal, but if you want it again it will always be there. Desire shapes your actions, therefore remember that while you have the desire you have the main requisite for success.

DISGRACE

We feel guilt because of our own actions, but we can feel disgrace because of the actions of others. A colleague of mine described how she watched someone she knew grow more and more haggard after her son had been sent to prison. Trying to comfort the elderly woman she said, 'Don't worry. The time will soon pass and he will be out again.' She received the answer, 'It's not that, doctor, it's the disgrace.'

It is not easy to comfort people made ill by such disgrace. We can tell them how passing time dulls people's memories; how a mantle of disgrace is ready for each of us if we care to wear it; how reparation and repentance can even the score. We can point out that our feeling is no more than a mixture of hurt and pride and fear of public opinion and that if we can rise above this and think of the feelings of the one who has disgraced us and who may be suffering far more than we, we shall have done a fine thing. We can do all this and find that the disgrace is still hard to bear.

If you are ill because of such disgrace, you have the compassion, not the censure, of every humane person. Also, those who love you will love you more, not less, because of your disgrace.

If your own actions have disgraced you, you have no alternative but to study where you failed and be determined not to do so again. And remember that most people like to see a disgraced person make good. It restores their faith in human nature. A few idle tongues will wag a little more than usual but their prattle is worthless at any time. Concentrate on your true friends. Take the encouragement they offer.

23. Obsession

While problem, sorrow, guilt or disgrace can start or play an important part in nervous illness, the side-effects of the continuous state of fear they may produce can also be distressing and may take precedence over the original cause. The most usual side-effects are:

- obsession
- sleeplessness
- that dreaded morning feeling
- depression
- loss of confidence
- difficulty in contacting people
- difficulty in returning home
- apprehension

The type of obsession experienced during nervous breakdown is characterised by repeated, distressing, compulsive thoughts or actions. The victim may suffer from more than one obsession and may, indeed, be in such a receptive state from fatigue that almost any repelling thought may cling and become obsessive.

In my experience there are three main types of obsession. One is simply a habit of repeating some ritual which is not so fearful in itself as the fear of the state in which the obsessed person finds himself. For instance, in the ritual of repeatedly washing hands for fear of contamination by germs, washing hands is itself not so frightening. The second type of obsession, however, holds much fear. For example, the very common obsession that a nervously ill mother will harm her child. The third obsession is shared by many sufferers from nervous illness. They become obsessed with themselves and their illness.

THE FIRST TYPE OF OBSESSION

The person continually washing his hands for fear of germs eventually comes to be as much alarmed at his compulsive state as by the imagined germs. This applies to all other obsessions of this type. It is as if one part of the sufferer's brain has lost its resilience, is worn out on this particular thought, so that he can no longer reason with it. This is frightening. A doctor may bring temporary peace to this patient, but it is not long before the old, well-worn tracks of thought and fear take over, despite the patient's efforts to resist them. Extreme mental fatigue on the subject seems to make it impossible for him to see any other point of view for long. This fatigue is not caused by obeying the obsession. One could wash one's hands all day without much fatigue, if one did so willingly. It is the tension, apprehension, exasperation and despair that accompany the hand-washing that tires. It is this *second fear* which keeps a brain non-resilient, tired, inflexible, and also keeps the sufferer so sensitised that his first fear, his fear of germs, remains unreasonable. *There need be no deep-seated cause for this fear of germs*; no cause that must be found before cure is possible.

The person with this type of obsession invariably makes the mistake of trying to fight it, stop it coming, forget it. He will never lose his obsession while trying so hard to do so. When he fights he merely emphasises the obsession and keeps it more vividly in his mind.

If you have this type of obsession, you must accept that it will upset you for some time to come. It must because you are so sensitised to it. But if you try not to be upset because you are like this, try not to add this *second fear*, you gradually remove the tension and thereby remove the fatigue that is keeping you sensitised. When you decide to try to accept your obsession willingly, you will find an inner peace and the obsession will not seem so terrible. Acceptance banishes the nightmarish quality of obsession. And when the second fear goes, your brain refreshes itself and you are then able to take the first fear, whatever it may be, more calmly, see it at last in its true perspective.

THE SECOND TYPE OF OBSESSION

As I said, this is a much more fear-inspiring obsession than the first. There is real panic in the obsession that a mother may harm her child. Understanding how an obsession like this arises is the key to its cure. I have explained so often how a sensitised person's emotional reactions to any upsetting thought are intensely strong, out of all proportion to the importance of the thought. When a nervously ill mother first had the thought that she could harm her child, it struck her with such overwhelming panic that at the height of the experience she let herself be carried away by the panic to a point where she became all feeling; she could not think. She did not follow the fear through and then think, 'Oh, yes. But I could never do that!' and at the same time feel that she never could. Had she done this, she would have ridden past fear and the episode would have been forgotten. Failing to do this, she became terrified of the experience and lived in dread of its returning. Naturally, arousing so much interest and fear, it returned; and each time it came she repeated the first mistake, until she established thinking and feeling this way as an obsession.

If you have this type of obsession, you must first understand that you have this strong reaction because you are sensitised and that you cannot be desensitised overnight. You must accept yourself as you are for the time being. Secondly, you must now do what you failed to do on that first overwhelming occasion. You must practise accepting the fear; but as you see it through you must try to glimpse the truth, which is, of course, that you would never do this thing. You are being bluffed by exaggerated feeling, bluffed by thought. Try to follow your fear reaction with the real, true point of view. You may only glimpse this at first, but with practice it will become stronger and stronger, until you will be able to hold it firmly and the obsession will gradually lose its meaning. You gradually replace the obsessive thoughts with the true thoughts.

I understand how difficult this is and know that such a person needs a doctor's repeated explanation and constant support and reassurance. It is a tremendous help if a doctor records each consultation on tape for the patient, who can then take the recording with her and so hear the explanation, listen to guidance, and receive encouragement whenever she feels she needs it; and this may be many times daily.

Obsession A person tortured by an obsession is in my experience always capable of understanding – if only fleetingly – the truth about it. For example, a woman obsessed with the belief that her house was contaminated with germs could glimpse the truth while I explained to her that there were few dangerous germs present in any house. I had cultures made from smears taken from each of her rooms, from her refrigerator, tap water, around her drain pipes and so on and they were all negative.

When she saw these results she realised that her repeated cleaning (the refrigerator sometimes three times in one day!) was unnecessary.

Yet, as soon as she left me, her reaction to the thought of germs returned so strongly, she was once more caught up in the obsession.

That fleeting moment when she saw the truth behind her obsession, I call 'glimpsing'. I cure patients of obsession by teaching them to practise glimpsing regularly and often. To do this, they sit quietly (or stand, it doesn't matter), think about their obsession and try to feel all the associated fear; then, while flooded in fear, *at that very moment*, to try to glimpse the truth behind the obsession, or simply to glimpse another point of view.

In the beginning, a mentally tired person (an obsession adds more fatigue to an already tired mind) may be able to glimpse only once or twice daily, but even one quick glimpse of the truth can expose the tricks that mental fatigue is playing and show that physical reaction to the obsession is severe because of sensitisation (the constant tension from obsession can be very sensitising) and not because of the importance, or truth, of the thought.

THE THIRD TYPE OF OBSESSION

Introspection may produce intense mental fatigue, which brings the sufferer a feeling of having his thoughts so bound within himself that even when he tries to be interested in other things he cannot free his thoughts sufficiently from himself to do so. He may try to work, talk, read, only to find his thoughts turning inwards every few moments. This may give him such a feeling of enclosure within himself that he becomes conscious only of his own actions, as if he cannot divorce his mind from them.

If caught in this way, you should:

First, understand that this obsession is no more than a symptom of intense mental fatigue.

Second, let your thoughts play their tricks as they will. Accept, as part of your natural thinking, even inwardly directed thoughts. Go along with them, think them. Don't be upset because you think this way and *don't try not to think this way*. Practise working while you think this way, until this habit *no longer matters*.

Understanding your condition as brain-fatigue that will gradually disappear with acceptance, understanding that you are not going mad and that many before you have felt the same way and have recovered by following the advice I have just given, will release you from much tension and fear: your thoughts will turn inward more lightly, will be less clinging, until they are no more than a touch, and the smallest interest will be enough to make you lose the habit. From time to time it may return. You must understand this also; but you will always know how to cope with it, and practice does make coping easier and easier.

To see an obsession as no more than habit born from fear and fatigue robs it of its fear-inspiring quality, and with fear gone only memory remains. Time fades memory.

A German woman with this type of obsession described it graphically and told how a friend helped cure her. When she felt one of these exasperating periods approaching, she would run to her friend and say, 'It's coming again, Maria. It's starting again!' and Maria would answer, 'Let it come, Anna. Don't try to fight it. Go with it and it will pass.' Wise Anna.

It is possible to cure some obsessions by removing oneself from the source of their origin. For example, a woman who had an obsession about crossing the main street of her town had occasion to leave the state for six months. On returning, she was delighted to find the obsession gone. Now, although she had lost her obsession she did not understand how and was thus vulnerable to its return. I want to teach you to understand obsession and cure yourself without running away, so that you will be invulnerable for ever.

So, to cure obsession:

- Accept and do not try to force forgetfulness.
- Stop fighting.
- Glimpse the other point of view.
- Let time pass.

Once more, the familiar pattern of recovery.

24. Sleeplessness

By nightfall some sufferers from nervous breakdown feel so much better and brighter than in the morning that they almost convince themselves they are cured. Others, particularly those with problems, dread the night. They lie in a bed of panic and sweat, with terrifying thoughts racing through their minds, waiting for sedation to calm them. They are afraid to be in the room alone and dread switching off the light.

If you are in this state, sedation is indeed a boon, but there are other ways to woo sleep.

First, understand that your fears are terrifying *only because your body is in a sensitised state*, shooting off exaggerated responses, where normally you would feel perhaps no more than a vague disturbance. *Your problems are not as terrible as your exhausted body would have you believe.* If you were not having such upsetting reactions at the thought of them you could probably cope with them. Therefore, try to see your panic for what it is, *the exaggerated response of an exhausted nervous system* and not necessarily an expression of the magnitude of your problem. Make yourself as comfortable in bed as you can, relax to the best of your ability, then examine the feeling of panic and be *prepared to let it sweep over you. Relax and go with it.* Do not shrink from it or try to control it.

You will find that if you can do this, the waves of panic will settle into being a hot, sore feeling in the pit of your stomach. You can get so used to this feeling that you can drop off to sleep with it there.

Your own thoughts may bring this panic, or it may sweep over you without apparent cause. If your thoughts are to blame, recognise that they are only thoughts, although, coming as they do so charged with fear, they may appear as monsters. Recognise that they are only thoughts and let them float away. *Release them. Let them go. Do not clutch them.*

When you decide to face panic and see it through, you feel some relief and this brings its own relaxation and a certain amount of peace. I say a certain amount, because at first you may not be aware of a great change in the way you feel. Although there is acceptance in your mind, your body may not respond to this for a while. However, it is possible that you may be surprised at the relief you feel. This may be so great that you may find your attention wandering from yourself.

It is easy for me to say relax and accept. I know that it may be very difficult for a tense, panic-stricken person to relax, but it can be done. Remember, the panic is there only because your nerves are sensitised to it. *One spasm of fear is making you more fearful of the next,* so that each spasm seems more intense than the last. If you relax, analyse the spasms (as advised in a previous chapter), and resign yourself to having them temporarily, you will develop an inner peace which will break the cycle of spasm–panic–spasm.

If unsolved problems aggravate your sleeplessness, you must act and do something about solving them or coming to some compromise. I have already suggested how to do this. Sleeplessness will not pass until you have a plan that will cope at least with your major problem. Indecision and conflict leave you a prey to fear and fatigue. Your mind may literally feel as weak as water. In trying to decide, it may turn first one way and then another, until you feel incapable of making any decision, and lie floundering, sweating and uncertain. It is this uncertainty, this constant hesitation between two paths, that makes you so vulnerable to panic and sleeplessness. Hence the necessity of having a point of view, found for you if need be, to which your mind can cling and so rest itself and find sleep.

HOW TO RELAX

Many articles have been written on relaxation. Therefore I will only briefly describe here a simple method, the nucleus of most other methods.

Lie comfortably in bed, first making sure that the bedclothes are not too heavy. Then, beginning with your feet and passing up to your legs, abdomen, chest, neck, head, arms and hands in that order, imagine that each in turn is so heavy it feels as though it is sinking through the mattress. Be sure to include your jaws and tongue in this lead-laden picture.

When you first relax your abdomen you may be more acutely conscious of its pulsation than when you were tensely controlling it. Understand that this pulsation is no more than the action of the main artery in your body, the aorta, in its effort to pump blood into your legs. If you press your hand into your abdomen you can feel this artery pulsating. Pulsating blood is your lifeline. Why be upset by this normal, necessary phenomenon simply because, as a result of tension, it is more forceful than usual and you are therefore more conscious of it?

The throbbing noise in your ear is also caused by blood coursing through one of the larger arteries in your head. When you hear this, instead of arranging your pillows to try and deaden it, say to yourself, 'There goes my lifeline. Good for it! Why worry if it's a bit loud tonight?' Relax and let it throb, and the pumping will calm down.

HEAD NOISES

Some people complain of a noise in their head like a pistol shot, which comes just as they are going off to sleep. Be pleased if you hear this. It is a sign that your tensed muscles are relaxing and that sleep is not far away.

Others say their head seems to swing on the pillow like a pendulum. This is yet another sign that sleep is coming. Rest your head on the pillow and let the pendulum swing. It is possible to fall to sleep with it swinging, and the pendulum does you no harm. It is but a temporary upset in your balancing mechanism caused by fatigue.

LISTEN

There is yet another way to find sleep. Sometimes a tired brain can be exasperatingly overactive. You can help to calm this excessive activity by using the receptive area of your brain, that is, *by listening*. Lie and listen to outside noises. Thoughts will come while you do this, but they will not be as penetrating as when you are actively thinking, nor will they be such organised emotion-bearing thoughts. I do this after a day of pressure when it is a temptation to lie awake and relive the day's happenings or plan the next day's activities. I simply lie and listen and have trained myself to do so for longer and longer periods without thinking. Sleep eventually comes. The well-known suggestion of counting sheep is an example of this principle. When watching imaginary sheep we use the visual receptive area of our brain and spare the thinking area. In practice, listening to outside sounds is much more effective than watching sheep, which few seem to find satisfactory.

Of course, I know there are people whose nerves are so agitated, and for whom stress is such torture, that sleep so induced would be too slow in coming. These people, if not given sleep quickly, face the next day more exhausted than when they lay down the previous night. They should consult their doctor about it.

But I emphasise that sedation alone will not cure. The patient must be prepared to *accept and float*, must have settled his problems or have found a compromise and must now be using sedatives mainly to overcome the residual tension in his body brought on by weeks, even years, of previous suffering and fighting.

THE JIGSAW PUZZLE

The person with a nervous breakdown has the habit of frustrating sleep by lying in bed at night trying to 'work things out'. He endeavours to unravel why such and such occurred today and to decide what he could have done to avoid it. I remember a woman who came to me late one night to tell me she 'had the answer'. She said, eyes bright with excitement, 'I know why my arms ache and keep me awake. I shouldn't have typed so much today. I overdid it.' She had spent hours working that one out.

Don't lie in bed trying to fit the pieces of your breakdown together, like reconstructing a jigsaw puzzle. You excite and disturb yourself unnecessarily, because you will make a different picture each night. You don't have to trace your way out of breakdown step by step. Practise masterly inactivity, and when you lay your head on the pillow at night try to accept everything and float off to sleep. If you do this, sleep will come in spite of your having typed too much during the day.

CHILDREN

A nervously sick mother with small children finds it difficult to get enough sleep. The children so often wake and demand attention just as she is drifting off. Noises heard as a tense person is on the verge of sleep can cause an electrifying reaction, disturbing, almost painful and capable of bringing the sleeper back to full consciousness in a matter of seconds.

I explain to husbands the benefit of uninterrupted sleep for a sick wife and stress that no woman with a nervous breakdown should have the responsibility of looking after children, especially at night. Unfortunately some men are difficult to convince.

The social workers at public hospitals can be most helpful in these circumstances, and in some cities a doctor's request can produce help free of charge from an emergency housekeeping service. However, I usually advise the sick mother to leave home for two months (not one), if possible, and not to think she is 'deserting the ship' by so doing.

If it is impossible for a mother to leave home or obtain help, she has no alternative but to accept her lot with as little frustration as possible, remembering that it is not so much rising and attending to the children that continues to keep her awake, as lying in bed afterwards burning up with the thought of how she would like to hang, draw and quarter every one of them, starting with the peaceful snorer at her side.

As well as philosophical acceptance, such a housewife has her relations, good neighbours and sedative to help her, and I have seen these work wonders. She now also has this book.

OTHER STRANGE HURDLES

Going to sleep may be beset by other strange hurdles. If the sufferer has had a series of sleepless nights and feels another would be more than she could bear, the very intensity of her desire for sleep is enough to make her more tense and anxious, and this becomes so upsetting that sleep is even less likely to come.

The principles of treatment stressed here meet this and each of the emergencies described above. Relax to the best of your ability, and accept the strangeness, the previous loss of sleep, the palpitations, the tension, the sweating, the panic, remembering that behind all this *Nature is waiting to put you to sleep. Sleep is lurking in the background, even behind such tension.* Also remember that if sleep does not come tonight it will come tomorrow or the night after. It will eventually come. It has been coming nightly to humankind for thousands of years. *This habit is stronger than your power to prevent it.*

By this I do not mean that you should lie awake for hours waiting for sleep to come. It is wiser to take a prescribed sedative and cut short the hours of tension. The frame of mind described above can be cultivated while waiting for the sedative to take effect or when you have improved and are beginning to sleep without sedation. Remember, your sedation must be prescribed and supervised by a doctor.

So, to encourage sleep:

- Understand that your fears are terrifying because your body is in a sensitised state.
- Relax, and let panic sweep over you, go with it, do not shrink from it.
- Recognise that much of your panic is inspired by thoughts and do not be bluffed by thoughts.
- Settle your problems as soon as you can, seeking advice, if necessary.
- Remember that head noises are harmless.
- If your mind is overactive, lie and listen to outside sounds.

- Do not excite yourself at night trying to unravel your breakdown; practise masterly inactivity, relax and accept.

- If you have done too much during the day, don't waste energy lying in bed worrying about it.

- Remember that the habit of sleeping is stronger than your power to prevent it. Do not hesitate to use sedatives, but remember that they must be prescribed by a doctor.

25. That dreaded morning feeling

Waking in the morning deserves special attention. It is the worst time of day to most people with nervous breakdown, not only because it brings another day to face, but because it may also so disappointingly fail to fulfil the expectations of the previous night. There are days when the sufferer feels comparatively well and by evening has convinced himself that he really is getting better at last. He goes to bed cheerful and optimistic only to find, on waking the next morning, that the previous day's improvement seems but a dream.

It is strange how the morning has this disconcerting habit of apparently paying little regard to the improvement of the day before. People are disappointed and bewildered when, after going to bed fairly cheerful, they wake the next morning to find the same old heart of lead, the same depression, the same churning stomach, the same difficulty in facing the day, the same desire to switch off their engine and pull the blankets over their head. It is as if the morning lags behind the pace of their recovery.

It is not easy to find a satisfactory explanation for this dreaded morning feeling. It may be that consciousness steals upon you before you have time to marshal your defences. If you have had oblivion in sleep, the moment of waking, bringing the return of cold reality, may strike like a blow across the face and your spirits may sink before you have time to save them. Or, it may be that sleep relaxes an overtired body to a point beyond normal relaxation and this is as hard to bear as tension. Whatever it is, I do know that when you wake in the morning feeling that the world is not such a bad place you are well on the way to recovery. The suffering felt on waking must be understood, almost expected, but not magnified. Don't let it bluff you. *A difficult morning need not mean a difficult day.*

RISE WHEN YOU WAKE

To cope with this morning feeling, *you must rise as soon as you wake.* The longer you lie steeped in misery the harder it will be to pull yourself out of it. I fully understand how difficult early rising can be, but it can be done, even though it may mean literally dragging your body out of bed. 'I leap out of bed,' said one woman. But very few people with nervous breakdown are prepared to leap out of bed. It is enough if, as soon as you open your eyes, you rise, however slowly, have a shower and then go and make a cup of tea. You will find that cheerful music helps to lift you out of the early-morning doldrums, so have a radio beside your bed. The family may not appreciate an early-morning concert, but when they know it is part of your treatment they usually co-operate.

After music, shower and tea, you can lie more peacefully in bed until the family stirs. You may prefer to go for a walk rather than return to bed. So much the better. The main thing is *to make some quick effort as soon as you open your eyes, so that the early-morning depression cannot establish itself.* Having done this, you will not so easily slip back into depression again. At least it will not seem so overwhelming as it might have done had you stayed in bed with the blankets over your head. Be prepared to greet the mornings this way until waking becomes easier and you know you can lie in peace without the aid of music, shower or tea.

When I advised one young woman to rise as soon as she woke, she remonstrated, 'But the bodily functions aren't working! How could I get out of bed before the bodily functions work? It sometimes takes hours for mine to get going!' I assured her that her 'bodily functions' would work more quickly in response to command than to coaxing, especially when their owner lay in bed engrossed in the coaxing. Admittedly the first half-hour may be deadly, and it is from this that most people shrink. However, after a while the way becomes easier, helped by the prompt rising.

So don't listen to any excuse you may make to yourself to lie a little longer. *Leave that bed as soon as you wake.*

HAVE COMPANY

Having someone congenial to talk to on waking is a great comfort, and do not think yourself a coward if you would like some member of the family sleeping in the room with you. This is good treatment and I sometimes advise it. To see another person on waking brings a feeling of reassurance and reality and a few spoken words can be as balm to a troubled mind.

At least place your bed so that you can see out of the window when you wake and are not forced to look at the same spot on the ceiling, or at the same old dressing-gown hanging up behind the door. To see something moving outside, if only the boughs of a tree, is a distraction, and somehow helps you to feel more normal.

EARLY-MORNING SEDATIVE

If you wake at four o'clock or thereabouts, it becomes a problem to decide whether to take another sleeping pill, get up, or just lie and 'stew'. Even though the family may be willing to suffer the disturbance, four o'clock is too early for you to begin the day. You are left with too many hours to fill in until the household stirs. So I advise patients to take a little more sedative. For this purpose, a tablet is prescribed which acts quickly and yet does not leave much hangover. Even if you do not sleep again, the tablet is calming and you can more easily lie and wait until it is time to rise. When I advise rising as soon as you wake, I do not mean to do so while the moon is still shining and the owl still sitting on the fence.

All so quiet in those early hours – so still To a nervously ill person who wakes in the very early hours, the quietness can seem threatening; even the sound of the early-morning garbage van is welcome. At least someone is alive! And, oh!, the relief of hearing movement in the house, especially the rattling of cups and saucers!

I once mentioned early-morning quietness to a patient from the country. She laughed and said, 'Oh, doctor, you've obviously never lived in the country! You should just hear the animals at our place and the sound of heavy boots stomping around the kitchen at the crack of dawn!' Perhaps the sound of heavy boots is comforting someone at this moment.

Noises that come regularly at a set time – for example once or twice a week – can be a yardstick to gauge progress or lack of it. Every Tuesday when the garbage van calls, the rattling cans can bring hope, or the despair of 'another bloody Tuesday!'.

Sometimes the early-morning waker can be so anxious to return to sleep and blot out those hours of waiting, she becomes wider and wider awake.

In my opinion there is a stage in nervous illness when an early-morning sedative may be necessary. It may be better, if the sufferer is agitated, to shut out those early hours of lonely suffering, than to have him exhaust himself trying to live through them – accepting one minute, being overwhelmed the next.

However, waking later – at about five o'clock or after – is no time for a pill. At this time it's better to wake right up, listen to the radio, read, get a hot drink. Taking a sleeping pill at five or after can make the body feel even heavier when trying later to heave it off the bed to face another day.

A CHANGE OF VIEW

You may be surprised how helpful it is to change your bedroom or even the position of your bed or the curtains in your room. To wake each morning and see the same curtains with the same pattern, of which you know every detail, reminds you so vividly of all the other mornings of suffering that you may seem to be dragged back into the quagmire before you can save yourself. Change refreshes – even such small changes as these. As mentioned, change acts like a mild shock which temporarily arrests your attention and draws it away from yourself and so helps you to feel more normal. Even a short respite from suffering is heartening.

So, should you wake with that dreaded morning feeling:

- Rise immediately, have a shower, make a hot drink, find some cheerful music on the radio, or, if time permits, go for a walk.
- Do not be too impressed by the necessity to lie in bed until your 'bodily functions get going'; rise and get them going yourself.
- Place your bed so that you can see outside on waking.
- Change your bedroom if possible; at least occasionally move the furniture in your room to make a change.
- Above all, accept and do not be discouraged by the mornings while waiting for them to improve, remembering that a difficult morning need not mean a difficult day.

26. Depression

A person emotionally exhausted by months of fear and conflict may become apathetic, with little interest in his surroundings, or he may feel a more overwhelming desperate and powerful physical feeling of depression, a sickening heaviness in the pit of the stomach. It is said that the stomach is the most sympathetic organ in the body. It weeps when other organs are sick. It is certainly the focal point of depression.

Depression is one of the worst phases of nervous breakdown because it robs so many of their wish to recover. However, there are still those who can rise sufficiently above it to hope for recovery, *however deep their depression*, and that they can do so organically.

Modern anti-depressant drugs (when used temporarily and when tailored to the individual) can help greatly, but these, like sedatives, should be prescribed only by a doctor.

OCCUPATION

Although occupation is discussed in detail in a later section of this book, it must be specially mentioned here because it is the mainstay in the treatment of depression.

To cure depression, BE OCCUPIED, KEEP OFF THAT BED IN THE DAYTIME!

I emphasise the *importance of occupation in the company of others* for depressed people. I have seen such people on the verge of recovery deteriorate severely when suddenly deprived of occupation. If depressed, *do not attempt to recover by sitting about the house watching the days pass, trying to fill in each as it comes.* You must have an organised program so that you can look ahead for days, preferably weeks, and know that your time will be occupied. I find it difficult to convince a patient's family of the importance of this. They have no conception of how long an idle hour can seem to a sufferer from nervous breakdown. His tired mind, turned inward on itself, is conscious of every second as it passes, so that an hour seems an eternity and tension increases until it becomes almost unbearable. This situation is exasperating to a doctor to observe because she knows that idleness, tension and depression make a most formidable combination, which could have been avoided had she but had the family's co-operation.

It is absolutely necessary that thoughts be claimed by outside interests, so that time passes more quickly, the strain is eased and depression relieved.

SMALL, HAPPY, DAILY EXPERIENCES

Normally our spirits are kept up by small, happy, daily experiences of which we are hardly aware. For example, while we wash up and try to decide whether to make the beds next or hose the garden, we handle the smooth china we like and notice the sun shining on the scarlet geraniums on the window-sill. Our heart lifts up, and when we go into the bedroom, it is with much less than our usual annoyance that we remove the sleeping cat from the bed. The person with a nervous breakdown if shown a garden full of geraniums would probably stare and say, 'Geraniums? What geraniums?' Her preoccupation with her problems and herself deadens her powers of observation and so bars entry to these small joys.

So many of these small, happy experiences are waiting to help lift your spirit. The future is not as black as you may think. You do not need some great happiness to bring back joy in living. The little things will do that, as soon as you have eyes to see them.

THE LONELY PEACE OF SOLITUDE

Working out of doors is particularly recommended for depression. The brightness, the expanse of sky, the absence of restraining walls, the movement, all help to keep spirits raised and troubles in proportion. The depressed person with no inner source of joy for support depends almost entirely on a cheerful environment to help him. A melancholic atmosphere is almost unendurable. Indeed, his reaction to sadness is so exaggerated that a slightly depressing situation may seem tragic to him. And this reaction is quick. A nervously ill woman went to stay at the seaside. She arrived at dusk on a windy, grey day. As she stepped from the automobile a gusty wind from the beach brought the sound of the local amateur band practising mournfully near by and a handful of crows circled overhead calling their baleful 'Caw! Caw! Caw!' The depressing effect was instantaneous and shattering. She felt her heart sink into her boots and she said it took two days of sunshine to recover it.

It is often better for a depressed person to sit in the local movies or have a meal in a busy shop or restaurant than to rest in the lonely peace of solitude. Brightness and diversion help to hold the interest and support the flagging spirit.

RESPITE MAY HIGHLIGHT SUFFERING

Some people with nervous breakdown refuse to visit the movies for several reasons. They say that the feeling of unreality they experience there makes them more aware of the frightening, unreal feeling of their breakdown. Others say that to hear so many people laughing happily only emphasises their own isolation and misery. While others find that although they can lose themselves in a movie, to come back to the hard light of reality when the performance is over and face their breakdown again can be such a contrast, such a shock, that their illness seems more overwhelming and hopeless than ever. The respite only highlights their suffering.

It is such strange experiences as these that make nervous breakdown a bewildering maze and keep it alive as a constant source of torture. To get out of the maze you must go forward and meet these experiences when they come. Do not try to avoid them, but do not challenge them and seek them out unnecessarily. Merely accept them and be prepared to let more time pass until you can face them without suffering. Remember, the blow that strikes as you are recalled from temporary forgetfulness of your suffering is *no more than a thought*. YOU ARE BEING COWED BY A THOUGHT. Do not be bluffed by a thought. Why not try to think a comforting thought instead of a frightening one? This may not be easy at first, but practice makes it easier. Instead of thinking, 'Dear God, the breakdown! Will I never escape?' you can think, 'I was able to forget for a while. That's good. I'll forget about it altogether in time.' Recognise how much of your breakdown is built up from *no more than frightening thoughts*. Float past them. You can with practice.

Facing your breakdown after momentarily forgetting it is an experience you may have to go through daily. This will be less and less painful each time you face it with acceptance and hope and the breakdown itself will seem less and less overwhelming. But I do not mean that you must face every particular detail of breakdown that frightens or depresses you. It may be wiser to avoid certain experiences, especially if facing them serves no useful purpose. For example, one woman had had an especially depressing, upsetting nervous experience at the movies and she said that she now had only to see the outside of a cinema to have devastating reactions. She had made herself worse by going especially to the movies 'to try and conquer' this feeling.

I explained that her reactions were severe now only because of present oversensitisation of her adrenalin-releasing nerves and that visiting the movies in the future would not always affect her this way. While it was necessary for her to face, unmask and then float past fears that must be met, going to the movies served no useful purpose at the moment and it would be better to avoid such unnecessary suffering until her reactions calmed down. But I emphasised that she must avoid *sensibly*, *hopefully*, *not fearfully*, knowing that eventually she would have only a memory of her earlier disturbance. She must realise that avoidance now was merely to save reopening *a healing wound*. She would not recover so quickly if she fearfully avoided the movies, or if she went there tensely prepared to 'fight this thing'. Can you appreciate the difference between these two approaches? It is one of the keys to recovery.

LIVING ALONE

When they are well, people live alone successfully because they have the energy and interest to take part in the life about them. When in breakdown, living alone may seem unbearably tragic and depressing. I strongly advise you not to live alone while having a nervous breakdown. By all means leave home temporarily and stay with friends or even go to a boarding-house, anywhere where you can live with people. But do not make any arrangements now to permanently relinquish your home. You will feel differently about it when you are recovered, and homes are not easy to find. Make no impulsive, irretrievable step.

DEPRESSION IS YOU, NOT THE WORLD

Also, a depressed person should remember that depression is a physical feeling expressing the extreme tiredness of his emotions. As you stop flogging yourself with fear, fight and flight from fear, you become less tired and depression gradually lifts. Your body is like a car with a flat battery. If you keep trying to turn the engine over the battery has no chance to become recharged. If you can float without flogging your body with fear and worry, it will recharge itself with *joie de vivre*. Depression does not last for ever. Float past this period of depression, looking hopefully ahead.

Above all, remember that depression is you, and it is not the world that is so terrible. Depression is an illness, just as influenza is an illness, and Nature is waiting as readily to cure one as the other, if you will let her. But depression works in such a vicious circle: the memory of yesterday's suffering makes such a bad start for today. You can get outside that circle by saying, 'All right, yesterday was a bad day. Today may not be good either, but as the days go by, they will gradually improve if I let them.' When you can say this and mean it, you will see a miracle happen.

Remember:

- However deep your depression, you can recover.
- Depression is a temporary illness.
- Modern anti-depressant drugs can be helpful.
- Keep off that bed in the daytime and be occupied in the company of others.
- Have a planned program of occupation.
- When respite highlights suffering, review your thoughts and substitute hope for despair.
- Once more, depression is an illness; Nature is waiting to cure you.

27. Loss of confidence

The person with nervous breakdown invariably complains of loss of confidence. Indeed, many say that they feel their instability so acutely that it is as if their personality has disintegrated. This feeling is fostered by the sufferer's bombardment by quick, fierce flashes of emotional reaction to the slightest unpleasant stimulus. This assault, in the presence of a stressful situation, is so disconcerting, even overwhelming, that its victim cannot rise above it to think clearly. In addition, he is usually so mentally tired that thoughts come haltingly, accompanied by headache. Because of this, he is indecisive and vulnerable to suggestion. He feels no inner strength on which he can depend; no inner self from which he can seek direction. It is this lack of inner harmony holding his emotions, thought and action together which leads him to choose the word 'disintegration' to describe his condition.

Old-fashioned sayings can be surprisingly apt when describing nervous breakdown. For example, the saying 'pull yourself together' describes so well what such a person feels he should do. It is as if he must gather the scattered pieces of his personality together and fit them into place before a confident, integrated person can emerge. To do this he usually has to overcome the very weakness in his character that helped to cause breakdown, so that as he recovers he is integrated on a higher plane, is a better person. Hence his acquisition of new confidence.

A young doctor came for help. He had lost confidence after a series of domestic mishaps, and his nerves were so tired from fear and worry that his work suffered. To give a simple injection became a battle. Each day was spent fighting such battles until he was sure the work was too much for him. He panicked and wanted to give up medicine. He used the term disintegration when describing his state.

I explained the cause of his apparent disintegration and emphasised that he could continue successfully if, instead of meeting each situation with tense determination to overcome it, he were to relax, accept his present condition as temporary and float past the reactions aroused by any aspects of his work that now dismayed him. In other words, to do his best as calmly as he could and be satisfied with the results, recognising that to expect more from himself in his present exhausted condition would be foolish. I explained fully the meaning of 'float'.

The young man returned later, a different person. 'I have learned the trick of floating,' he said. He told me that his first experience on returning to hospital had been trying. He had been obliged to give an anaesthetic which, in his nervous condition, had seemed particularly difficult. To make matters worse the surgeon, scalpel in hand, had turned to him and said, 'I suppose, young man, that you know this patient has a weak heart?' The young man was on the verge of laying down his tools when he recalled my words. He knew he was capable of giving the anaesthetic, so he floated past the destructive suggestion that he could not do it, reminded himself that this was only a thought, released it and quietly went on. He had no more trouble.

I do not advise all sufferers from nervous breakdown to stay at their posts, particularly at such a difficult one as this. Each person's problem must be assessed, and it is sometimes wiser to leave work temporarily.

Do not be alarmed by the term disintegration if you have not heard it before. Your personality has not truly disintegrated. Your adrenalin-releasing nerves are merely oversensitised by fear and continuous tension, and your mind slowed by fatigue. This creates the illusion of disintegration. When your emotional reactions calm, you will quickly feel integrated again. You are now passing through a very temporary phase. Integration and confidence return together. One depends on the other and both depend on peace of mind.

What causes setbacks? A setback usually comes in two stages: first, a sufferer's sensitised reaction to some disturbing circumstance or memory, and then his alarm at the return of the old familiar nervous symptoms.

While some sensitisation lingers, stress can trigger the return of many, if not all, of the old symptoms. If the sufferer understands and accepts this, they gradually subside. However, if he becomes afraid and tense and thinks, 'Here I go again! I'm going to slip right back!' and stays afraid, he opens the door to setback. It's the second fear – the fear of setback itself that he adds – that can entrench him in setback.

A sensitised body can continue to react intensely and swiftly to stress even when the sufferer understands and has reached a stage where the symptoms no longer upset him. Physical recovery so often lags behind understanding and acceptance that it's good to be prepared for an occasional flash of sensitivity; being prepared is the best defence. More time must pass; the way is always on and through, always onward.

With enough practice going into, and out of, setback, setbacks may threaten, even come, but they no longer frighten, and when a setback no longer frightens, it passes very quickly. Indeed, it is no longer a setback – it is not even a halt – it's simply an accepted, even expected, experience on the way to recovery.

A NEW FEELING IS BORN

In the beginning you may not be able to follow confidently the advice given in this book, firmly grasping your nettle. *The most to be hoped for at first is that you decide to try to do as shown.* You will find that the decision in itself will give you a new feeling, admittedly a little shaky at first, but nevertheless a new feeling will be born. Your confidence grows and hope comes into the picture as you see the method work. The return of confidence plays a big part in determining the rate of your recovery. Remember, the power of a muscle can depend on the confidence with which it is used.

You may despair again and again. This is not important if you remember never to despair completely and are always willing to pick up the pieces and go on. If you do this, you will one day feel the confidence you need so much. It will be born from your relaxed acceptance of all the strange sensations associated with your breakdown and the determination never to admit defeat. When I said this to one woman she said, 'How can I never admit defeat?' The answer is that you are never defeated while you are ready to go on.

UPS AND DOWNS

The road to recovery is beset with many temporary failures. It is like travelling across the foothills toward the mountains. You travel downhill so often that it is difficult to realise that, in spite of this, you are still climbing. This up and down aspect of recovery is exhausting and frustrating. I remember one young man saying, 'I'm tired of being up one minute and down the next. I'd almost rather stay down all the time and be done with it!'

It is true that just when you think you have turned the corner and are feeling well, you can have one of your worst setbacks. You can waste much energy trying to discover why this happens. A patient will say, 'I had a wonderful week last week, doctor, the best yet, and then on Saturday and Sunday I felt terrible, as bad as ever. How is this possible?'

It may have been some trivial event that drew her back, but is it so important to find out? Strangely enough, it always seems so to the sufferer. Actually, it is important only to realise that tomorrow is another day and could be the best yet, however upsetting yesterday or today may have been. Do not measure your progress day by day. *Looking forward hopefully with confidence is a tremendous help. It draws you past the yesterdays, past today, past the tomorrows, until you find recovery.*

The slipping-back process is easy to understand. The past holds so many fearful memories for the person who has had a nervous breakdown, even a slight setback will find a host of them ready to engulf him. It takes time to dull these memories. But after he has pulled himself out of a few such reverses he despairs less readily, and confidence grows from each experience. When you have achieved confidence by your own effort, nothing can take it away again. No future defeat can quite destroy it. It may seem in moments of despair that it has gone, but the memory of past successes, however small, gives you the courage to try again, and so defeat is defeated.

So, recognise that:

- Disintegration is no more than bombardment by exaggerated emotional reaction accompanied by slow, confused thinking and is caused by emotional and mental fatigue.

- Integration will return with peace of mind and peace of body.
- Confidence is born by going on despite defeat.
- In spite of ups and downs on the road to recovery, the main direction is upward.
- Confidence earned from your own experience will never leave you completely.

28. Difficulty in contacting other people

So many people with nervous breakdown not only complain of loss of confidence but also that they do not feel part of the world about them. It is not unusual to hear one of them say, 'I cannot make contact with other people. It is as though they are in one world and I am in another. However hard I try, I don't seem able to find my way back into their world. Am I going mad?'

When desperately concerned with our own problems, it is not easy for any one of us to be interested in a neighbour's new automobile. It is even more difficult for the person with a nervous breakdown. It is this narrowing of interest experienced in breakdown that leads to a feeling of withdrawal from the rest of the world. It is not easy to contact people if, while talking to them, one's mind is continually reverting to oneself. Also, for the person with breakdown this world of introspection is charged with such intense suffering that it is impossible for him to feel in tune with anyone who can laugh light-heartedly. Introspective suffering has withdrawn him from the world of normal living and he will not feel part of this again until his interest is in it and not in himself.

This feeling of inability to be part of the world around him is accentuated by his impatience to step straight out of his world into normality; that is, by his impatience for quick recovery. The transference is usually gradual. It may take weeks for him to be sufficiently interested in everyday life to feel part of it.

NORMAL EMOTIONS FROZEN

The illusion of loss of contact with other people can be so strong that some people complain they can feel no love for those they used to love, even for their own children. It is as if they have a vacuum where their feelings should be. Such a person has merely complicated his feeling of withdrawal by exhausting his capacity to feel normal emotions. He has felt fearful emotions too intensely and too long.

It is a mistake for this person to search for, and try to force normal feeling. He must wait for it to return as it inevitably does. It is as if his normal emotions are frozen and he must wait for them to thaw. One woman in particular complained that for months she had felt no contact with her husband and two children. After six weeks' treatment away from the family, they were due to visit her. She immediately began to worry about whether she would feel closer to them now. I explained that she was making an issue of the situation by worrying so much about it. She had thought she had lost contact with the family for so long, the habit had become established and it was most unlikely that she would find it changed in six weeks, especially while she watched the situation so anxiously. *She must be prepared to wait for more time to pass and not record and demand progress from herself each day during their visit.* Actually, reconciled to waiting longer, she would be freed of much tension and anxiety and might therefore surprise herself by finding that they were once more all happy together.

IMAGINED STRANGENESS IN THE BEHAVIOUR OF OTHERS

Because of a feeling of withdrawal a person with nervous breakdown may feel so much outside the family circle that her imagination can fabricate a most emotionally involved situation from little. The woman just described, as well as thinking herself unable to contact her family, had imagined that the children no longer wanted her and would even be better off without her. Given enough time she was likely to project herself into a variety of odd situations.

I pointed out that the children's behaviour only reflected her own. They felt strange because she was acting strangely by being so conscious of, and making them conscious of, everything they said or did. If she could bring herself to be just 'Mum', help with their homework, talk with their friends as she used to, and cease analysing how they felt and acted toward her, they would soon settle gratefully into being the natural children they had always been. This was what they wanted most.

TOO MUCH CONTACT

In contrast with a lack of contact, some nervously ill mothers complain of being too aware of the family. They say, 'It is not fair that the sick mother should be made to feel that everyone else's happiness depends on her. Why must it always be the mother's effort to make happiness for everybody? Why can't they try to make me happy for a change? As soon as I get ill they all go to pieces!'

The answer is simple. When mother is well, she is the cord that binds the family together. When she is ill the cord slackens, the family feels at a loose end and keeps looking to her to put things right again. They never think to change places with mother and do a little cord-pulling themselves. They just sigh miserably and wait for the hand that rocked the cradle to start rocking again. I said to one young girl, 'There's plenty of food in the refrigerator, so what are you grousing about?' She answered, 'I don't like just going to the fridge and getting something to eat, I like having Mum with me while I eat!' When she is well this is mother's life and that is how she wants it; when ill, it is still mother's life and that is how she gets it!

TALKING ABOUT YOU

It is easy for a person with nervous breakdown, because of a feeling of withdrawal, to become sensitive and suspicious. He may think his friends are talking about him, and they sometimes are. They notice his strained, unkempt appearance, his absentmindedness, and they worry, so that when he re-enters a room he has just left, it is quite likely that sometimes the conversation will cease abruptly.

Do not be disconcerted by, or question, what you think is strangeness in the behaviour of others toward you. Accept it all. Shrug your shoulders and think, 'I am not going to be silly. It will all come right in time. Time will fix it.' It will.

Look ahead to the peace of recovery and let time carry you there.

So:

- When you walk through the streets wondering if you will ever be in the same world as the passers-by, remember that you will be there just as soon as you lose interest in your world of fear.
- Do not try to force normal feeling; let time bring it back to you.
- If others seem to act strangely toward you, practise shrugging your shoulders.

29. Difficulty in returning home

It is often advisable to remove the patient to new surroundings to help speed recovery. However, the time eventually comes when recovery is sufficiently advanced to warrant returning home. Perhaps you are in this situation and the thought of going home hangs over you like a dark cloud. You think, 'How will I react to being home? Will I slip back?' If you are returning after recovering by floating and accepting, you will have an excellent idea of how to act, because the same principle applies. There must be no fighting; no spotlight turned onto your feelings; no questioning yourself, 'Do I like this? Do I like that?'

It is not important how you feel when you first go home. Your feelings are bound to be mixed. You will be glad to be home; frightened to be home; scared of seeing again the places where you suffered; glad to be among the people you love and yet afraid lest you disappoint them and become ill again. *Realise that none of these feelings is permanent, and that none is therefore really important.* Admit them to yourself, but do not make much of them. Accept that you will probably have a strange mixture of feelings for a while. Who wouldn't? Talk about them with a sympathetic member of the family. Putting your fears into words will help to dispel them more quickly. But deep down, take with you the knowledge that *reconciled acceptance of all strange feelings will gradually abolish them.* You have already experienced how acceptance has calmed the sensations of breakdown. It will also calm these feelings of apprehension.

Despite your resolutions, you may seem to deteriorate on first returning home. You may be left alone all day, and after being constantly with people while away, the contrast with the loneliness at home may at first seem too great. Also, in spite of preparing yourself for distressing memories around the house, actual contact with them can be surprisingly upsetting, and you may fail to differentiate between reality and memory. So that, as you wander from room to room, assailed by painful recollection, you may panic and think you are 'slipping back'. You think, 'Why can't I be happy in my home? Why must it do this to me? I'm no better than I was. And yet I felt so much better while I was away. What's wrong with me?'

This is the home you love, but it is also the place where you suffered deeply and it would not be humanly possible to forget such suffering easily. You may remember the woman who said she couldn't get a 'hold' on herself. Eventually she was cured and after a holiday telephoned joyously to say how well she felt and that she was coming to see me the next day. She arrived looking well enough, but did not seem as radiant as she had sounded the day before. In fact, she wore the shadow of the old frightened look and I said, 'You're surprised to find that as soon as you sat in that familiar chair, your old fears came back?' She answered, 'They were back before that, doctor! As soon as I put my foot on the stairs, they were back! What's wrong with me?'

I said, 'You would be a magician if you could immediately banish the memory of suffering associated with climbing those stairs. But understand that *it is only memory* and don't be bluffed by it. Float past it, and the next time you come you will be surprised how easy it will be.' She left relieved and happy.

So, if faced with a similar situation, accept that you may be at first disturbed by painful memories on returning home, but float past them, realising that as the days pass, these memories will become fainter and fainter, until they are replaced by happy ones. Also, as this happens, the knowledge that you are recovering brings its own joy and relief and helps you to forget past suffering. To sit peacefully and talk to a friend will at first be a wonder and a delight. Gradually you accept it as part of normal living, and that is how it should be.

Sometimes, perhaps weeks, even months after returning home and when you have forgotten the sharp edges of your breakdown, some reminder of it may catch you unawares and momentarily bring back some of the old sensations. At first you may be frightened and think, 'Oh, not again!' But you will then remember that you cured yourself in the past and will realise that you could do the same again if need be, and your fears will calm and you will think, 'Why bother to let it all start again?' And you don't bother. You float past the upsetting reminder.

Your inner core of confidence is there, firm as a rock against any destructive suggestion. This is your security against all further nervous breakdown. You understand and therefore are unafraid. You know the way in, but you also know the way out. YOU WILL NEVER BE LOST IN THAT MAZE AGAIN. YOU HAVE BEEN RESCUED FROM BEWILDERMENT.

So:

- Return home with confidence.
- Recognise the difference between memory and reality.
- Do not be bluffed by memory.

FACING AGAIN WHAT MADE YOU ILL

It is very encouraging if, when you are about to return home after recovering from breakdown, your family says, 'Everything's been changed at home. We understand what made you ill. You won't have to face that again.' You can now sail home with all flags flying. But more usually the family says, 'You've been away for months. You should be cured by now. So the sooner you can come home, the better.' No mention of changing anything.

Removal from the source of trouble allows time for emotions to calm, so that when you think of your problems your revulsive reactions are probably less severe. You have had time to acquire a certain insulation which helps you to 'rise above the situation'. To put it another way, your exhausted adrenalin-releasing nerves, removed from the source of constant irritation, have had time to recover and no longer shoot off exaggerated responses at the mere thought of your trouble. You can think without too much feeling.

So far so good. But simply to return calmer and hoping for the best is not good enough. You are too vulnerable. Underneath your newly acquired calmness you are wondering how long your new suit of armour will last without cracking. To feel more secure you must take home a definite plan of action. You must have an acceptable way of looking at your problem before you return.

If your past suffering was severe enough to cause a nervous breakdown and if, on returning home, you must face the same source of suffering it is obvious that you must have very good reasons for returning to it. The natural inclination is to run in the opposite direction.

If you are going home simply because there is nowhere else to go, possibly because you have no money and no training to earn money, and no desire to take an untrained job even though this may mean living in peace away from home, then admit that you are not a poor, persecuted human whose head fate insists on putting on the block, but a very usual sort of person who insists on putting her own head on the block. Stop regarding yourself as a martyr. With the martyr element eliminated, the situation at home will seem less intolerable. Somehow, what comes will not seem so bad when you admit that returning to it is really your own choice.

For example, if you are the mother of children returning to a husband who spends his evenings away from home and who comes home the worse for drink, then you are obviously going back because you have decided that he is not such a bad father when sober, and that it is better for the children to have a home with him in it than without him. So, instead of working yourself up while he is out at night, put his meal in the oven and find another interest. You have elected to make a home for the children so make it a home, not a battleground. It is amazing how once you change your way of looking at a situation, the situation itself may change.

So:

- Understand why you are returning home.
- Keep this firmly in mind.
- Take your head off the block and make the most of the situation.

30. Apprehension

THE SHADOW OF THE SHADOW

Although the person recovering from breakdown is no longer as afraid as he was, he may be unable to lose a feeling of apprehension. This perplexes him. He thinks, 'Why should I still have this vague feeling of anxiety, as if something terrible is about to happen? I have nothing to worry about now, why should I feel like this?'

This feeling is most likely to come when he first wakes in the morning, before he has time to review the now more cheerful aspects of the situation, and reorientate himself. It is an emotional habit, brought on by the months or years of true anxiety. It has been called the 'shadow of the shadow'.

Most of us have experienced this feeling. It is common in middle age when many become lost in sorrow. The health we accepted as our right, the body we have not had to worry about previously, may give us a nasty shock and we could find ourselves faced with one or more spells in hospital. Also, domestic troubles are most likely to come at this time. Parents must be nursed through long illnesses and lost in death. The growing family is at an age when they may cause grave concern and many nights and early-morning hours may be spent listening for the key in the door before sleep will come. Troubles may follow in such rapid succession that, even when absent, we feel as if they are hovering in the background waiting to return.

Time and acceptance alone can dispel this. However, they may take so long to do their work that the sufferer may seek a doctor's help.

The patient often describes herself (it is usually a woman) as feeling more 'flattened' than actually depressed or unhappy. She is easily discouraged. She thinks, 'Wouldn't it be nice to see Alice?' but when she considers bathing and dressing she doesn't want to go. If Alice could materialise and say a few words, she would quite enjoy it, but to dress and catch a bus? No, that is too much! Planning any pleasure ahead is a burden.

These people sometimes come to the doctor almost in tears. They think they have a real problem. How are they to become themselves again? Are they going mad? Or (hopefully) is this menopause?

Most people are greatly relieved to hear that they are no different from many others who have passed through this period of life. They are especially comforted to understand that their trouble is an emotional habit, is not mental and that they can be cured.

The cure is the same for you if, on recovering from nervous breakdown, you are left with a background of anxiety you cannot understand. You must lose the habit of carrying anxiety around. First, *make the effort to go and see Alice*. A habit must be broken, a shadow's shadow lost and the quickest way to do this is to replace it with other memories, other feelings. It is surprising how close to the surface normal feelings lie when you once make the effort to rid yourself of the shadow of the shadow. You might start out to see Alice feeling as if you couldn't care less if the bus were to go on to Timbuktu, but after Alice has talked about herself for half an hour and you have talked about yourself for an hour, it is surprising how much better you feel. On the return bus journey you may even find yourself moving up amicably to make room for someone.

It is not easy to find the same lift by staying at home and merely lecturing to yourself while waiting for time to pass. It is essential to get away from the house, where the shadow feels too much at home. It is essential to meet other people. Many middle-aged housewives go to work temporarily to help lose this feeling and they are so much better for the daily change of scene that that which began as temporary occupation becomes permanent.

You can also help to change the daily pattern of your feelings by spoiling yourself a little each day. For example, a housewife once wrote to a journal describing how she overcame such a condition by some small, daily self-indulgence. When she saw violets on the flower-stall, instead of thinking, as was her previous habit, 'Such a price to pay for violets! What an extravagance!' she bought them and made a point of enjoying them throughout the day, stopping to smell and admire them. She was changing the pattern of her emotions by purposely introducing happy moments. Indulge yourself in this way, so that you will grow used to the feeling of happiness again and it will gradually replace anxiety. Make the effort to help the shadow of the shadow pass and don't forget the violets.

31. Three good friends: occupation, courage, faith

By now you will appreciate that nervous breakdown is no more than emotional and mental exhaustion usually begun and maintained by fear. Most of us experience, to some degree, suffering of this kind during the normal course of our life, so that we could say that nervous breakdown is but an accentuation of such normal experience. There is no monster waiting to devour us; no precipice over which we will fall 'if we don't look out'; no special point beyond which recovery is particularly difficult. *Anywhere, at any time during breakdown, if we lose our fears, we can step out of it.* Perhaps not immediately, but in a surprisingly short time.

You may feel that fate is ready to push you back at every opportunity during your recovery, but you can be cheered by the thought that, whatever fate may do, three good friends will never fail you – occupation, courage and faith.

OCCUPATION

To a person with nervous breakdown idleness can be a torture, each moment an eternity and the strain almost unbearable. The exhausted mind races agitatedly and yet watches each second pass. No amount of self-chastisement can stop it. It seems almost beyond the powers of the sufferer to free himself from this situation, unless he has some crutch on which to rest his tired mind. *Occupation in the company of other people is his best crutch.* But it is essential that he is not still bewildered by his problems and is not throwing himself into occupation as a way of fighting them. This leads to greater exhaustion and more bewilderment.

This person must first *find some solution or compromise for his problem, seeking advice where necessary; he must be prepared to cease fighting and float forward to recovery, accepting all the tricks his nerves play on him while attempting to lose himself in occupation.*

While occupied, one can, as it were, divide one's mind into two parts: the part that suffers and a new part that accepts and floats on. In spite of this new approach, the part that suffers will probably continue to suffer to some extent, with trouble hovering in the background, *but in the background.* It is now that occupation is such a blessing. It claims attention and acts like a splint for the tired mind, replacing painful by impersonal thought, so that the suffering gradually recedes. I repeat *that this happens only when the emotional pattern is acceptance and looking forward to future healing without resistance, resentment, fighting and fear.*

Unfortunately, many people who break down are middle-aged, and it is not easy to find suitable occupation for them. Middle-aged women who have primarily been homemakers are more difficult to help than men. A man can often continue at his work, which usually provides a daily change of scene and company.

One middle-aged man had been representing his firm abroad on an undertaking which involved mental strain, competition, arduous travel against time, and little sleep. He became exhausted when he needed his wits about him and he panicked at the thought of failure. He completed his work and returned home, but by this time was well advanced in a nervous 'collapse', which he suffered for two years. He was given various treatments without lasting benefit and when I saw him he was desperate. He explained that he was so ill that each thought was a burden. This was particularly upsetting because his work as an engineer entailed intricate thinking. He had tried many times to return to work, but each time had given up in despair and had returned home a worse wreck than ever. Nobody, said he, could have fought harder. I showed him where he had made his mistakes and advised what to do. He said, 'What you say seems too simple. But I will try your way.'

As he was physically exhausted, I prescribed light occupation at home for a few weeks, reconditioning an old car. At the end of this time he was improved, but still afraid to return to work and risk failure. Once again I pointed out his mistakes in the past. I explained that his brain was not damaged, as he thought; that it was as capable as ever of complicated reckoning, but could work only at a slow pace.

I also showed him how previously, when he had begun to calculate, he had first put up a barrier of fear and lack of confidence. How could he expect a fatigued and therefore highly suggestible mind to overcome this and work satisfactorily? His brain was so exhausted by despairing thought, small wonder that it could only plod along. What a magnificent mechanism to function at all in these circumstances!

I pointed out that he must be prepared to attempt his engineering problems many times before he could solve them. He must accept that at the moment there may be some, perhaps many, he could not solve. *On no account must he make an issue of solving them, trying to prove to himself he could do it.* He must relax to the best of his ability, breathe quietly and calmly and be prepared to think as slowly as his tired mind allowed him. In the circumstances how could it think quickly?

Also, he must not worry about how foolish he might look to others. What matter they? Who knows, the day might come when one of them would knock on his door for help.

Again and again I explained that the quality of his thought was not changed, only its rate slowed by fatigue, born of tension and fear.

This man recovered after some months doing as advised. It was not easy, but no worthwhile success is easy. He is now a leading executive of his firm and a much more soundly integrated person than before his breakdown. What is just as important, he is no longer vulnerable. If his nerves start to play their old tricks, *he relaxes and accepts them*, does not attempt to fight them. Relaxation and acceptance give little encouragement to nervous breakdown.

This man was fortunate in that he had favourable conditions in which to recover. His position was waiting for him and he could return to it as gradually as he wished. Also, an understanding wife stayed beside him, even though at times she was hurt, frightened and bewildered. The doctor can do much if he or she takes the time to explain nervous breakdown to such a wife.

The situation between husband and wife can become complicated. The husband, if he is the sufferer, unable to make up his own exhausted mind, may turn to his wife for guidance over small details. Then, feeling himself a weakling for so doing, he will act against her advice in some pathetic effort to reassert his manhood and re-establish his dignity in his own and his wife's eyes. It is not surprising that some wives become desperate.

Middle-aged housewife

A man, with occupation normally away from home, usually keeps his trouble more in perspective and recovers from breakdown more quickly than a housewife who is left to make beds, sweep floors and wash up, with only children to talk to. There is little about the work to distract her. She does it automatically and in a place where she is constantly reminded of her suffering. It was while washing up that she had her first attack of palpitations, so the sink now holds new fears for her. Also, the families of most middle-aged women have left home, so that the housework is lighter, is finished by midday or earlier, and the woman is left with the long weary afternoon hours to fill in. She cannot always spend time with her neighbours, however co-operative they may be.

A lonely sick housewife described in writing how she felt after the family had left for the day. Her words are reproduced here without alteration. She wrote, 'A feeling sweeps over me. I get hot, my face burns, my throat keeps swallowing, my lips get dry and tremble, I cry and feel as though I am going to smother. My tummy is churning. I feel I don't want to be alone. I close my hands, they are tense. My neck muscles get tense. My legs get wobbly. My head feels tight and feels as though it is going to lift. I now want to clench my hands. I have sat down at the veranda table. This is something I have been unable to do before. Before when I felt this turn coming on, my first impulse was to go outside and walk about. I now feel a little better. My husband has gone. I felt awful when he drove away. I am going to try and be sensible and go inside and wash up and talk to my little dog.'

The next day she wrote, 'I woke up thinking I should go with my husband. But he could not take me. Later the feeling of being alone swept over me. Tomorrow they are going early. This seems to be a big problem. I get a feeling as though I am smothering and the walls are closing around me. I still feel tense and will try and do some housework. I will have to wait all day now until they come home. This seems a big problem.'

Surely it is obvious that this woman should never have been left alone trying to cope with those long hours before her?

If such a person is unable to leave home temporarily, it is most helpful for the doctor to visit the home and see the conditions under which the patient is trying to recover. I had advised the woman just described to sit on her porch rather than stay indoors and she had conscientiously done so, with little good result. I had not known, until I saw it, that the porch was enclosed by a high wooden partition and that, when seated, she could not see out. I requested that the partition be lowered immediately, but I first removed this woman elsewhere.

For the housewife, I try to find creative occupation, different from housework and yet not demanding too much concentration. It is sometimes difficult to convince a husband that it is better for his wife to attend a class in the making of artificial flowers than to be home cooking his dinner. 'If she can fiddle with flowers, why can't she cook supper?'

If you are a nervously sick housewife, do not feel guilty if you want to leave the dishes, make artificial flowers, breed dogs or dig in the garden. Housework is rarely interesting to a woman with breakdown, and since interest is the force that will help to lift you off the bed and out of breakdown, find it where you reasonably can.

A woman to whom I was recently called lay on a couch while being interviewed. She apologised for the state of the house, in particular for the state of the back veranda, saying that she had not the strength to work and that the veranda should have been painted months ago.

I suggested that she should start painting it the next day. She looked at me in amazement. How could she paint a house when she could hardly walk from one room to another? I could see her wondering what kind of doctor had been foisted on her.

I asked how long she had been on the couch and she answered, 'Three months.'

'Are you better for it?' I inquired.

She thought a while and said, 'No, I'm not. I guess that's why they've called you in.'

I assured her I was not joking about the painting, and asked her sceptical husband to assemble the necessary implements by the next day. She could begin by scraping the paint from one of the window frames. This was not as strenuous as it sounded, because I had noticed that the paint was already falling off in long strips.

I also assured her that it was not important if at the first attempt she could scrape for only a few minutes. *It was the attempt that was important*, the effort of getting off that couch and facing a new task. I explained that she could not damage her body making such effort, that indeed her muscles would regain their ability to function normally, *only if she used them*. Muscles that have not been used for some time always complain when first used again. Their aching is only their peevish protest, not a measure of damage done by their re-use. In fact, in spite of such aching they will regain their normal strength much quicker when used than when laid aside to rest.

When I called a few days later she was gently scraping the window frame, in between sitting on a chair strategically placed near by. A week later she was at the undercoat stage and we had a brisk discussion about the colour of the final coat. We settled for French grey walls and a Chinese red door. The thought of the red door acted like a magnet. She forgot her 'poor weak legs' and almost ran to the garage to find the paint to show me. The next week our conversation was more about the painting than the breakdown. She was cured by interest in doing something refreshingly different. Confidence in her own strength was restored by using it.

I am not saying that this woman's tiredness was imaginary and that all she had to do was to pick up her bed and walk. The tiredness of breakdown is real and may require some daily rest, but only a certain amount.

The sufferer may complain, and how often she does, that she is too exhausted to work. She is almost right, but only almost. Emotional stress may have reduced her to nothing more than skin and bone but, however weak she may be, she is better out of bed occupied somehow. The body will recover as the mind finds peace and the mind is more likely to find peace when occupied than when brooding. An hour spent in bed in panic will exhaust more than light occupation will. Your body is ready to obey any reasonable demand, however exhausted you may think yourself, provided your interest is in what you are doing and not in watching your body work for fear you may 'overdo it'.

An American doctor worked so strenuously in Greece after World War I that when the last day of her appointment came, and she was about to sail for home, she almost collapsed, saying she could not have worked another day. A few hours later she received a cable sending her immediately to work in South Russia. Now, her one regret on going home had been that she had not seen Russia. She became so interested in her new appointment that she started working at full speed and forgot to collapse. We are usually exhausted more in spirit than in body. However, I emphasise that your doctor must have examined you and diagnosed your trouble as 'only nerves'.

The patient is bound to overdo it occasionally, often in the beginning. It is not unusual to find him in a quandary trying to estimate how much work he should attempt so as not to overtire himself. My advice is always the same: while it is unwise to undertake tasks that are obviously too strenuous, it is better to work and risk overtiring yourself than to do nothing for fear of it. But it is important that when you do overtire yourself, you do not lose confidence and waste additional energy regretting and wondering, 'Why?' There will probably be many such episodes before you are completely cured. If you accept the fatigue calmly, rest and work again, you take two steps forward to each step back.

Organised occupation

It is always difficult for a doctor to find occupation for his patients. How much easier our work would be, and how few patients would need radical treatment, if there were places organised by the medical profession, where people harassed by nerves could be kept occupied and away from home. By such a place I do not mean a hospital where the patient mixes with other patients and the atmosphere is laden with talk of nerves, their treatment and complications. I mean such places as farms, schools, etc., that would be willing to find bed and occupation for some of these people, who would then be able to work and recover in normal surroundings. Much of the good that comes from hospital treatment for nerves is achieved mainly by removing the patient from familiar, distressful surroundings. Even to be away from the strain of being watched by an anxious family must be a relief.

I do not wish to decry the good work done by hospitals, but I do consider that a person with nervous breakdown who recovers in normal surroundings has a better chance of being more firmly integrated and more soundly rehabilitated than one who is treated in hospital. The one in normal surroundings is actually being rehabilitated while being cured. Also, it is better for his morale and needs less explanation to inquisitive acquaintances.

It is a great help if such a person can, like the engineer described at the beginning of this section, continue at his usual work while awaiting cure. Occupation is there, already found, and he does not have the strain of meeting any embarrassing situation that may occur on returning to work after a prolonged absence with nervous breakdown. Also, he quickly loses any feeling of strangeness that his illness may have brought him. Fitting into a normal pattern helps him to feel more normal. However, it may be difficult for him to remain at his usual work because he may find it too much strain to keep to a schedule. People with nervous breakdown can do a great deal at their own pace, but if asked to work to a fixed time or keep an appointment punctually, they may feel incapacitated by the strain of anticipation.

For example, the nervously ill mother of two small boys had progressed so well away from home that she was soon able to return each day to clean part of the house and help prepare the evening meal. When the school holidays arrived it became necessary for someone to be with the boys each morning when the father left for work. He expected the mother to be there. After all, she was well enough to do nearly everything else by now, why not come at eight o'clock each morning instead of drifting in at any hour of the day? What difference? His wife soon taught him the difference. She went to pieces at the mere suggestion. She simply could not take the strain of a set appointment. She explained that to know she must be with the boys by eight in the morning was enough to banish sleep the night before. She felt she could not tolerate the strain of waiting for the hours to pass until morning came and wanted to relieve it by rushing home immediately.

I try to impress on the family the importance of keeping such strain from the patient during the early weeks of convalescence. Sometimes they listen with disapproval. They think that if mother were obliged to do such and such she would be much better for it. If mother did such and such she would probably be better for it, but not if she were obliged to.

Finding suitable occupation is a problem that must be met and solved with each patient. I can but emphasise the absolute necessity for it. If further proof were needed, one has but to compare the patient of Friday with the same person on Monday after an idle weekend. So often there is deterioration. 'Sundays nearly kill me,' say so many.

There is a special type of isolation treatment, where the 'nerve' patient is put to bed in hospital and isolated from outside contact. This may work for some, but the risk is great. It is too much strain for a tired mind to be thrown on its own resources for hours, days on end. I repeat again and again, be occupied. LET OCCUPATION BE YOUR CRUTCH.

Do not misunderstand and feverishly seek occupation, fearing to be idle. Moderation in all things, even here. Occupation can be interspersed with rest. But it is better to err on the side of too much activity than too much rest.

The company of others is just as important as occupation. Some years ago a young man described an illuminating experience he had had while recovering from nervous breakdown. He was staying with friends in the country where he was obliged to be alone most of the day. One of the friends was unexpectedly home for two weeks, so that, for the short time, the sick man had continuous companionship. At the end of the fortnight he was much improved and he described how desperate he felt when he knew that had he had company for just a few more days, the rest this would have given his tired mind would have been just enough to allow him to find the command over his thoughts he so desperately sought. As it was, he had the distressing experience of watching himself slip back and lose some of the ground gained, knowing there was little he could do but accept the situation philosophically and wait for more time to pass.

This man should have had occupation with daily companionship and not a quiet country holiday. Quietness is often mistakenly prescribed for 'nerves'. It may be easier for some people to recover from nervous breakdown in the noisy distractions of the city rather than in the still, pressing solitude of the country.

So:

- Let occupation be your crutch.
- Accept all the tricks your nerves play on you while attempting to lose yourself in occupation.
- Relax, accept the temporary slowness of your thought and be prepared to think as slowly as your tired brain allows; time and peace will bring full recovery.
- If you are a housewife, do not stay alone all day; find interests away from home.
- Seek occupation in the company of others.
- Remember, an hour spent in bed in panic will exhaust you more than light occupation will, so get off that bed.

Resting on the bed in the daytime 'I get a lot of help from your books, but I can hardly agree when you say, "Keep off that bed in the daytime!" I get so very tired doing my level best to carry on with every nerve crying out loudly to rest. Someone rang me just now and the shock of the telephone nearly killed me. I have suffered all my life with nerves and some of your advice has helped a lot, except that bit about keeping off the bed in the daytime. Oh dear, I thought I could cope with it better. I was going to tell my doctor how much you'd helped me until now! If you could possibly write and explain what you mean by keeping off that bed in the daytime, it would certainly be a help.'

This woman is seventy and recently had an accident. Her wounds became infected and she was in hospital for weeks and had to return there for further treatment. Of course, she should have rested on the bed or couch in the daytime. This is an example of how careful and explicit a doctor should be when speaking or writing. I thought I was careful but I wasn't thinking of victims of accidents.

Others have been puzzled by my statement about keeping off the bed in the daytime. When I made that statement I was thinking of nervously depressed people who would take to bed as a refuge and lie and brood on their illness, convinced that they hadn't the strength to get up and do anything about it. Also, I thought of the nervously ill person who would lie and worry about his problems and rise later feeling worse than when he lay down. A pillow makes a too encouraging nest for a head full of worry.

Of course, people who know they will benefit from daytime rest (as this woman obviously did) should take it. No question.

COURAGE

Courage has the extraordinary quality of being there *if truly wanted*. If you want, earnestly enough, to be courageous, you will be. If you fail, re-examine yourself and you will find you have misled yourself. You only thought you wanted to be brave, you did not actually feel the urge. To be conscious of a real urge, you must feel it strongly within yourself, in the pit of your stomach, so that you can almost put your finger on the spot. In other words, this wanting must come well forward in your consciousness, and not be tucked away, overlaid by wishy-washy wishing.

You must establish and cultivate this feeling until you make it part of yourself. There is nothing difficult or illusory about this. It is almost a trick, like the trick of floating. Lie still and close your eyes and think of something you want very much, something for which you have a deep yearning. It is here, where you feel this yearning, that you will also feel courage and confidence: always the pit of the stomach. In the beginning be satisfied if you feel only a yearning for courage. If you persevere, with practice it will become courage itself. But first make sure that you feel it. *Feel the yearning* in your stomach, *do not only think it* in your head.

It is unfortunate that our training does not help us to bring such positive inner feelings more easily to our assistance. When young we are taught to do, think and feel, until we react to the pattern laid down by our training. Our true selves, our real possibilities, we rarely uncover, and we can and usually do go from cradle to grave without knowing what we, the true you and I, honestly think, believe or feel.

So do not be satisfied with the mere wish you may now feel to be brave and persevering. Give your desire so much concentration that you eventually make it a granite-like determination to succeed. If you take time to do this, your journey to recovery will be winged.

It is curious how this feeling of courage and confidence seems to be seated not in our brain, but in our 'middle'. This is a good place to feel it, it adds strength to our 'backbone'.

A doctor has a unique opportunity to see examples of great courage. After years of practice, the average doctor emerges with respect and love for his or her fellows. They have their faults, but their courage makes these faults so easy to forgive. An old patient of mine, a woman of eighty-two, suffered one of the most trying illnesses known. One night, after she had had a particularly gruelling day, I went into her room expecting her to be in despair. Instead, I found her listening to the radio and reading from a book of short stories.

I said in amazement, 'I did not expect to find you cheerfully reading like this.'

She looked at me quizzically and answered, 'What's the use of crying in the dark?' This book is dedicated to the memory of that patient.

To get such courage *you must want it*. When you finally have it, it will stand between you and all future adversity, between you and failure. Find it, as I have suggested, and if you lose it, search again. And there will be no more crying in the dark.

FAITH

The religious have faith in God to help them. But those who are not religious find little comfort in being told to put their trust in God and pray for help. They would of course recover if they did as this kind of faith is one very clear path to our version of facing, accepting, floating and letting time pass. But even those with such faith sometimes have to be shown the actual steps to recovery. Sometimes religious people think they are being tried by God or tempted by the devil, and they fight all the harder, to justify themselves before the one and master the other, only exhausting themselves in the effort.

The person who bears his suffering with patience (letting more time pass), and resignation (acceptance) and faith that God will cure him, has found a way to recovery, but many get lost on the way and forget how to apply their faith.

Again, some nervously sick religious people complain of being unable to contact their religion, like the mother who could not contact her family. This is an added worry, especially when they find no solace in prayer. When they understand that they feel this way simply because their emotions are exhausted, they are greatly relieved.

So, to tell people to put their faith in God and let Him cure them works only for those who have such faith and know how to apply it. These are indeed blessed. The others must be shown another way, or locate the same kind of recovery through their own, non-religious spirituality.

32. Dos and don'ts

1. Do not run away from fear. Analyse it and see it as no more than a physical feeling. Do not be bluffed by a physical feeling.

2. Accept all the strange sensations connected with your breakdown. Do not fight them. Float past them. Recognise that they are temporary.

3. Let there be no self-pity.

4. Settle your problem as quickly as you can, if not with action, then by accepting a new point of view.

5. Waste no time on 'What might have been' and 'If only . . . '

6. Face sorrow and know that time will bring relief.

7. Be occupied. Do not lie in bed brooding. Be occupied calmly, not feverishly trying to forget yourself.

8. Remember that the strength in a muscle may depend on the confidence with which it is used.

9. Accept your obsessions and be prepared to live with them temporarily. Do not fight them by trying to push them away. Let time do that.

10. Remember, your recovery does not necessarily depend 'entirely on you', as so many people are so ready to tell

you. You may need help. Accept it willingly, without shame.

11. Do not be discouraged if you cannot make decisions while you are ill. When you are well it will be easy enough to make decisions.

12. Do not measure your progress day by day. Don't count the months, years, you have been ill and despair at the thought of them. Once you are on the road to recovery, recovery is inevitable, HOWEVER PROTRACTED YOUR ILLNESS MAY HAVE BEEN.

13. Never accept defeat. Remember, it is never too late to give yourself another chance.

14. FACE. ACCEPT. FLOAT. LET TIME PASS.

IF YOU DO THIS, YOU MUST GET WELL.

33. For those who fear further nervous illness

If you have had a nervous breakdown you probably dread the thought of some day experiencing it all again. Most of these people say, 'I hope I never have another breakdown.' Very few have the confidence to say, 'I will never have another breakdown.' I want you to be able to say, and know, that you will never break down again.

If you are afraid of future breakdown, you probably avoid thinking about it and are content to bury the thought of it at the back of your mind and hope for the best. *This is not good enough*. In this condition you are subconsciously tensed and therefore vulnerable. If asked what you fear, you would probably hesitate and then list a number of dreaded possibilities, each related to your unhappy experience. I want you to be able to look clearly into the future and know that *your only enemy is fear*. Fear alone makes you vulnerable. Without fear there could be no future breakdown. IT IS AS SIMPLE AS THAT. Nervous breakdown is only an expression of sustained fear. *Its symptoms are no more than the exaggerated physical expression of fear.*

So, first appreciate that *it is fear and fear alone that can disarm you.* You are not obliged to fight the thought of having another breakdown in order to avert it. You need not bury the thought of it at the back of your mind. You are not obliged to watch lest you become overtired and so make yourself more vulnerable to breakdown. To be freed from all possibility of future breakdown, you have but to unmask fear, expose it, analyse it, understand it, and recognise what an all-important part it played in your last breakdown. Understand that *without fear your adrenalin-releasing nerves lack the stimulus to excite your organs to produce the sensations of breakdown.* You remain calm, and no one has ever had a breakdown while calm.

Scientists have devised tablets to tranquillise the action of the adrenalin-releasing nerves in the hope of preventing threatened breakdown. But you can produce your own tranquillity, your own invulnerability, if you do not shy from the thought of future breakdown, but face it squarely and see what can be done now to prevent it later.

There is much you can do. First analyse your previous breakdown and honestly try to find its cause. This may not be easy, because you may have to search well beyond the previously supposed cause. I have no doubt that you will find that fear was the real cause. Having done this, review your breakdown in the light of this discovery and consider how you could have solved your problems had you not succumbed to fear. There was a solution, wasn't there? While you consider this, you may for the first time face your previous breakdown honestly and may feel surprising relief.

Now consider the future and ask yourself what you would do if threatened by a similar situation. Would you let fear play as big a part in it, as you did before? I doubt it. Especially since you now recognise that *unafraid you would be invulnerable to breakdown.*

To be ever surer of freeing yourself from the bondage of fear, practise further unmasking it, 'debunking' it. The next time you feel a spasm of fear, instead of shying away from it and trying to forget it or to control and prevent it coming, as you have done in the past, I want you to examine it as it sweeps through you and even to describe it to yourself, noting in detail its various component sensations.

When you do this, you will find that the wave of fear strikes hardest when it first strikes, and that if you stand your ground and relax, *it quietens and disappears.* When you have learned to face fear this way, and see it as no more than a physical feeling, *you begin to lose your fear of fear.* You step outside a vicious circle. A spasm may come from time to time, but you learn to disregard it. Eventually it means so little that you hardly notice it in passing.

That niggly feeling: could the symptoms return?

A man wrote, 'Although I feel I'm almost cured, will I always fear that all the niggly symptoms could come back?'

The niggly fear will linger so long as the thought of a return of symptoms brings apprehension. When a sufferer is close to his past suffering, memory can bring a very vivid picture of those upsetting experiences. Small wonder that memory becomes accompanied by apprehension and a nagging dread that 'it' may return.

The writer said that he is almost cured. To be so near cure he has surely learned how to accept and so quieten some nervous symptoms. He can do this again. He should encourage himself with that thought, and instead of staying tensely on guard, trying to keep setback at bay, he should face the niggly fear and be prepared to let the symptoms come, full blast if necessary. If he does this, the niggly fear will gradually subside. The subsidence is quicker if he has an opportunity, not once but several times (even more than several), to pass through the return of symptoms successfully. Always, no-longer-mattering holds the key that brings future peace with no more niggling fear.

I said 'no more niggling fear'. However, the truth is that even when the return of symptoms no longer matters, carrying niggling fear can become a habit and can persist for some time. Once again, acceptance and letting time pass are joint healers.

LET THE FIRST SHOCK PASS

Now let us see how your conquest of the physical feeling of fear can affect your chances of avoiding future breakdown. If you were able to convince yourself that fear was the main reason for your previous breakdown (there will be no doubt of this if you are honest), you can surely understand that it did so by interfering with your power to think rationally. Can you see how, uninfluenced by fear, your ability to think and act would be so much more efficient? You would be able *to let the first shock* pass and then cope with the problem.

In the earlier part of this book I advised floating past fear. This is another way to express the advice just given in this chapter. By 'floating' I mean letting the wave of fear break and sweep past you, while you carry on in spite of it. When you can do this, you will retain your ability to think calmly, and calamity can never completely overwhelm you again. There can be no future breakdown.

I do not mean that whenever you feel a wave of fear approaching you must meet and analyse it. As you lose your fear of fear, these spasms will mean less and less and you will lose interest in them. If one comes more fiercely than usual you will accept it and not give it undue attention.

After you have practised as suggested, you will gradually understand and begin to feel the confidence you need so much to help you face the future calmly. Never forget that *without fear, you are invulnerable*, HOWEVER OFTEN YOU MAY HAVE SUFFERED NERVOUS BREAKDOWN IN THE PAST.

34. Advice to the family

The family of the person with nervous breakdown often accuses them of being a complete egoist. Many mothers complain, 'If I could be more sure my daughter were ill, and not just selfish, it would be much easier to put up with her. But, doctor, she is completely wrapped up in herself. It doesn't seem to matter to her that she has exhausted me and brought us all to the verge of breakdown with her!'

Perhaps you feel this way about some member of your family. If you have found time to read this book, a new understanding should help you to forgive such apparent egoism.

An author or composer in the throes of creating is so engrossed in his work that he may hardly be aware of what goes on around him and may so take for granted the comfort and peace provided by a pair of hands in the background that he fails to notice how lonely, neglected and even fed up the owner of the hands may be. A perfect egoist, but simply because of such demanding absorption elsewhere.

A person with a nervous breakdown is a somewhat similar type of egoist. In the beginning, his breakdown was probably caused by some disturbing fearsome problem, the continuous contemplation of which exhausted him and brought such alarming bodily sensations that other people's troubles seemed non-existent in comparison. Had he let himself become too aware of his family's concern about him, the added strain would have seemed unbearable. So, in self-defence, he shied away from such awareness, even to the point of appearing callous and egotistical. In addition, his needs are usually accompanied by such a strained urge for immediate appeasement that in his agitation to get relief he is quite capable of ruthlessly brushing aside the needs of others.

If you can see this relative as a sick person who, when well, will be no more egotistical than the rest of us, it will help you to tolerate and aid him now. Of course, if he was always selfish and his present state is but an accentuation of this, it is more difficult to tolerate him. Even here, show compassion for someone whose suffering is real and desperate and do not begrudge your sympathy or help.

SYMPATHY

The family is often warned against sympathising with the sufferer and unfortunately may take the warning too literally and be too hard on him. Do not be afraid to sympathise and show that you are trying to understand. Sympathy and understanding can comfort and encourage a wrecked spirit and relieve tension. However, do not encourage self-pity. Mix sympathy with a reminder that his problems are out of proportion and that as he improves they will not seem so insuperable. Above all, help to find, as soon as possible, a solution or compromise for those problems, and so save him from exhausting cogitation. It is the everlasting worrying, thinking and feeling intensely that is exhausting him.

If the problems cannot be solved, at least help him to find a less distressing way of looking at them and living with them. You may both have to discuss a new point of view many times before he can see it and hold it as his own. Try not to lose patience, however often he returns for such discussion.

OCCUPATION

Make sure that the sufferer is kept occupied. By this I do not mean that you must direct her back to work whenever you see her idle. I mean have a program of light work organised, so that it is ready for her. She may work only fitfully in the beginning, for her staying power will be limited. This is not important. But it is important that the occupation is there and that she is not left continually idle. An idle hour can be an eternity for her.

If your relative is a housewife, on no account must she be left alone all day. All the sympathy and help in the world given in the evening will not compensate for a day spent in the house with no company other than her own thoughts. I must repeat and insist on the importance of occupation in the company of others, particularly for a housewife, and ask you not to procrastinate in finding it.

Many families are willing to pay the expenses of a relative's illness but fail when it comes to finding occupation for her. This is so frustrating because the doctor can bring the patient only to a certain point of recovery, where occupation is essential to complete it. I explain this to every family and yet at each visit so many find some fresh excuse for not having done as requested. Please make every effort to find satisfactory occupation for your relative.

It is a great temptation when casting around desperately for a suitable sanctuary for your sick relative to think of Auntie Maud who lives three hundred miles away at Bargo Bargo in a dear little cottage on the side of a hill overlooking a river which leads, after half an hour's walk, to another dear little cottage on the other side of the hill. It is a great temptation to think that the peace and quiet, the lovely fresh air and the fresh cream will just fix Mary. Unfortunately that's just what they might do, but not the way you want Mary fixed. Mary may need company, change, distraction, constant diversion and not the lonely sound of the Boobook owl however fresh the air around it. To sit for an hour and sip a soft drink in a busy café and watch people come and go will help many people with breakdown much more than the fresh air in the lonely silence of the mountains. Depressed spirits depend so much on outside environment to help them. They have no inner source of joy to support them. They are like a weathercock that must turn this way and that with every changing breath of wind. In a sad lonely atmosphere the spirit can sink to a depth of despair understood only by those who have experienced it. So, if your sick relative has chosen to go to the country but writes imploring to come home after having been there but a short time, bring her home without complaining.

MOLEHILLS THAT CAN BE MOUNTAINS

If your relative has a particular problem that you can solve, however trivial it may seem to you, solve it. For example, a nervously sick woman had two prize dogs about which she was worried. Her husband promised to board them with a veterinary surgeon while she was away. When the time came to do this, he could not bring himself to spend so much money on two dogs, especially as it was needed urgently elsewhere. So, thinking he was acting wisely, he did not keep his promise. The wife, who was progressing well, as soon as she heard that the dogs were still at home worried so much that the results of three weeks' psychotherapy were endangered. I tried to show the husband that of all the money he was spending at the moment, that on the dogs was perhaps the best spent, wasted though it might seem to him.

I have described this incident because you may have a similar problem from time to time and may wonder why you should 'give in' to your relative. Do not regard it as giving in, but as saving mental and emotional suffering when emotions are so exaggerated and vulnerable. What may seem a molehill to you is a mountain to the sufferer. However, I do not mean that you must placate this relative at every turn. If you use common sense mixed with gentle firmness, understanding and sympathy, you will make few mistakes.

'FIGHT IT!' 'PULL YOURSELF TOGETHER!'

Never tell your relative to 'fight it'. Tell him not to fight it, to accept it; to practise masterly inactivity and float past troublesome issues that cannot be resolved; to float past fear of the bodily sensations of his breakdown. He must float, not fight. This is the way.

Also, should you advise your relative to pull himself together remember that you are talking to a sick person with a personality so affected by breakdown that to pull himself together would be literally to cure himself. You are, in reality, saying to him, 'For goodness' sake, cure yourself, quickly and now!' I know of no advice more depressing to such a sick person than being told to pull himself together, because part of the breakdown is trying to find a way through bewilderment to do just that. So should you use this phrase, at least appreciate what you demand and be prepared to show your relative how to do it. He doesn't know. Do you?

Do not think that by saying, 'Stop all this nonsense and go back to work!' you have shown him the way. Try to understand that to find the way to stop all 'this nonsense' is his biggest problem. So much of the nonsense has become conditioned reflex action, and who has ever succeeded in quickly stopping that?

It is true that sometimes going back to work is enough to cure nervous breakdown. It does this by helping to take the sick person's mind temporarily off his problems long enough to refresh it so that he can face the problems with less emotional reaction. Also the normal atmosphere of his daily work highlights the unreality of his breakdown and gives him encouraging flashes of normality to which he can cling.

However, taking problems and fears back to work is often of no avail, and the patient may be severely set back by the added indignity of having once more to leave work and return home ill. He may have made, in his opinion, a 'fool of himself'. It is safe for the sufferer to return to work only when he has a program of recovery planned such as is outlined in this book. With a plan to support and guide him, he runs little risk of failure. So, I repeat, when you say, 'Stop all this nonsense and go back to work' be sure you first show your relative how to stop the nonsense. I hope your compassion and interest have been aroused enough to prompt you to read this book carefully and learn how to help him.

35. What kind of person suffers from nervous illness?

Anybody is capable of having a nervous breakdown, although some will break (that is, fall victim to fear) more readily than others. Anybody given enough strain, sorrow or conflict is capable of exhausting himself, and if he makes the mistake of becoming afraid of, and trying to fight, the manifestations of his strained nerves, he can easily be caught in the circle of fear–fight–fear that leads to breakdown.

People can be helped or hindered by their early training. A child who waits at dusk, tense and afraid, for a drunken father to come home will not have the same calm nervous system as a child brought up in a happy family with parents who see that it goes to bed early and has a good night's sleep. Also, the child who is kept on the *qui vive* by an excitable parent is more easily aroused to exaggerated nervous reaction when the occasion arises than a child who is kept calm. Hysterical excitement is not good for the young. Let them look forward to happy events with pleasure, but not with exaggerated excitement. A calm word from Mum or Dad can do much. For example, instead of saying to the child, 'Only two more weeks to Christmas, isn't it exciting?' how much more soothing and sensible to say, 'You have two whole weeks before Santa Claus comes, so there is plenty of time to enjoy something else meanwhile.'

MODERATION

At school we are taught history, mathematics, etc., but rarely how to practise moderation and self-discipline. This is left to our parents to teach us, many of whom do not understand the meaning of the words, let alone their practice. Moderation and self-discipline are the most important part of our defence mechanism. The mature person can be moderate in all things, can free himself from emotional dictation, and act after suitable deliberation. It is difficult to act uninfluenced by feelings. If any one of us has to brush aside unpleasant emotional reaction to think reasonably, he finds it difficult to pass that emotional barrier. We are so often afraid of unpleasant feelings. We suspect that they may become more unpleasant if we face them, so we try to extinguish them before they become established.

Unpleasant feeling is particularly unwelcome if we have been allowed to grow up with our feelings meaning too much to us, because an indulgent parent has quickly substituted what we liked for what we did not like. If like this we usually want quick release from unpleasantness and rarely wait for our emotions to calm before acting.

If our education had included training to bear unpleasantness and to *let the first shock pass* until we could think more calmly, many an apparently unbearable situation would become manageable, and many a nervous breakdown avoided, because nervous breakdown is, as I have stressed in this book, no more than emotional and mental exhaustion following prolonged possession by unhappy and fearful emotions. The Chinese have a proverb expressing this. They say, 'Trouble is a tunnel through which we pass and not a brick wall against which we must break our head.'

A certain amount of suffering is good for us, particularly when young. We should not be sheltered too much. The experience you gain from your present suffering could be your staff in the years to come.

36. Dr Weekes speaks

Talk given as guest speaker at the Fourth National Phobia Conference sponsored by the Phobia Society of America and Phobia Clinic, White Plains Hospital Medical Center, New York, 7 May 1983.

As we all know, there are many different ways of treating nervous illness. I am speaking now of anxiety states with, or without, obsessions, phobias.

I recently read a book in which the author described most of the common methods of treatment of nervous illness used today. While they seemed different, they each claimed a good record of success. Whatever the treatment, in my opinion, success will depend on the sufferer's attitude to it.

If he is convinced that it will help him, the chances are it will; you know the saying, 'Nothing is but thinking makes it so.' However, in my opinion, a treatment based mainly on belief in it is in danger of working only temporarily. While the person treated continues to believe that it will work, he's probably safe; but let him begin to doubt any outside crutch on which he depends, and he's in danger.

For recovery, the sufferer must have, deep within himself, a special voice that says during any setback or dark moment, 'It's all right; you've been here before. You know the way out. You can do it again. It works, you know it works!' That voice speaks with authority and brings comfort only when it has been earned by the sufferer himself, and it can be earned only by making the symptoms and experiences that torture *no longer matter*. No-longer-mattering is the key. It is not a question of some method of treatment spiriting misery away, anaesthetising it. It is a question of the symptoms, the experiences, no-longer-mattering.

The necessity for the sufferer himself to earn the inner voice of assurance does not exclude outside help – for example, by giving understanding and direction and if possible by alleviating difficult, stressful circumstances.

The person alone all day with no program of recovery to follow, no special interesting work to do, who has somehow to fill each hour (the exhausted housewife struggling to cope with the housework, perhaps with a couple of children dragging at her skirt), the person who thinks himself too ill and weary to work, and who *is* ill and weary, with adrenal glands depleted by too intense and too frequent stress – what a mountain such people have to climb to earn that inner voice, especially if panic and other symptoms come by merely thinking about them.

These people's minds are all geared ready to thwart, ready at every turn to put up a barricade. The mind will remember and remind, mock, tantalise, never leaving the body alone. It will twist, turn, spiral, cavort – always turning inward, inward, inward, clinging with tentacles of glue.

And yet, all through this turmoil, the right comforting voice is there to be discovered. However, the sufferer needs to be shown how to make this discovery, how to make his torture no longer matter. It is not enough to simply have it subdued. Balance must be struck between the sufferer doing the work by himself and being helped. So the question is: What outside help should be given?

Some of you are, I know, sceptical of my using the word *cure*, especially if I had said permanent cure. I am aware that many therapists believe there is no permanent cure for nervous illness. When I was on radio some years ago in New York with a physician and a psychiatrist, the psychiatrist corrected me when I used the word *cure* and said, 'You mean remission, don't you, Dr Weekes? We never speak of curing nervous illness!' I told her that I had cured far too many nervously ill people to be afraid to use the word.

I suppose that were we to say that if a person saw a murder committed before his eyes, there would be no hope of his completely forgetting it, we would be right. I think that perhaps that is what some therapists mean when they say nervous illness cannot be cured, only relieved. They believe that memory will always return and that the nerves of a once nervously ill person may respond to memory with such intensity because of their past experience, that the poor devil is doomed. I think maybe that's what they mean. Also, I suspect that some therapists who deny cure of nervous illness may think, 'Once a weakling, always a weakling.' Maybe.

Of course, memory is always capable of recalling nervous symptoms, and what a heyday an anxious inner voice has then. It says, 'It's all back again! Every lock, stock and barrel. Every member of the family! We're all here. What are you going to do now? You'll never recover now, you know?' What power the wrong voice holds. But if the right earned voice is there it will come to the rescue and say, 'You've been here before, you know the way!' Then, in spite of being possibly shocked and temporarily thrown off balance, the owner of that inner voice does know what to do and gradually does it.

And that's what I mean by cure: having the right inner voice to support and lead through setbacks, through flash moments of despair, through bewilderment. That is cure. I don't mean that the once nervously ill person will always be at peace, will not have setbacks. Of course he may; surely he's entitled to be human. I mean that for a person to be cured, he must be able to take setbacks as they come (and they may come unexpectedly thirty years or more after the original illness), must take the setback directed by an inner voice that is the real tranquilliser. This is my meaning of cure.

And after each setback that inner voice is strengthened, and what is more, each setback successfully navigated by that voice reinforces confidence and self-esteem. Can you see how important, almost essential, setbacks are when the right inner voice is being developed to be the guide?

I suppose it's a lucky person who goes through life without being nervously ill. But I wonder. A person who has been nervously ill has widened his understanding, his power to appreciate, to feel compassion, even to enjoy.

Of course he has to carry the scar of memory. You know the saying, 'Where ignorance is bliss, 'til folly to be wise.' But if the sufferer has developed the strong, right inner voice, there is not so much folly for him in being wise. Without the right voice, all is left to chance, and that's very chancy. Also, the person who has been 'cured' (and I put 'cured' in quotes) by chance, by luck, by some outside crutch on which he continues to depend, can know only the peace of ignorance and that's no peace at all. It is only a temporary quietness. As long as his luck holds, he's probably okay. But luck has a habit of changing. It's a fool who trusts his life to luck, and we *are* talking about people's lives.

So I believe that in the work I have done I have tried to show the patient how to develop the right inner voice. The person who recovers using the four concepts that I teach – facing, accepting, floating and letting time pass – has done so by *going through hell the right way* and so has developed that right inner voice.

But in doing so, he has put his head on the block, has had to put himself into stressful situations that he otherwise would have avoided. And that's where he often falters, even sometimes fails. However, I teach him to know that peace lies on the other side of panic, on the other side of failure – never on this side.

There is a clinic in Toronto, Canada, specialising in treating nervous illness, whose superintendent wrote to me and asked permission to use phrases from one of my books. He said he had these printed on ballpoint pens which he gave to patients. One of the phrases chosen was: 'Recovery lies in the places and experiences you fear.' And that, in my opinion, is exactly right. I teach my patients never to be put off by the places and experiences they fear. These are their salvation.

The person who ventures into these places and experiences will of course sensitise himself more than if he avoided them; so I come to the question of drug therapy.

For some people I prescribe temporary medication, but, of course, I tailor the dose to the person. I always bear in mind that to earn the right kind of inner voice, the sufferer must go through his experiences acutely enough to learn that facing, accepting and floating do the real work. He would never know this if he were continuously medicated. As I say, the question of drug therapy is a delicate one and must be tailored to the individual.

There are people who can, and prefer to, go through the greatest hell without medication; however, the majority want, and need, to be helped with medication during the most severe stages of their illness.

Nervous illness is so very tiring. There is not only muscular, emotional and mental fatigue, there is also a kind of fatigue of the spirit, when the will to survive falters. I have found that when people reach this stage, to sedate and let them sleep even for a few hours can make all the difference. It can refresh enough for them to find the courage and strength to go on once more.

In my opinion, this is one of the main uses of drug therapy – to relieve fatigue and also to take the sharp edge off suffering, when suffering becomes almost too great for a body to bear.

I say almost, because there are those who can and do bear it. However, we should never demand this unreasonably from our patients. As I say, medication must be temporary and tailored to the individual.

So I leave you all with a suggestion: those of you treating nervous illness should find out what the inner voice of your patients is saying. In my opinion, when we think we have cured a patient but have not helped him earn the right inner voice, we have not cured at all, whatever method used.

If some of you suffer from nervous illness, find out what your inner voice is saying. Be honest about it. Face it. If it brings no reassurance, find a voice that does – by facing, accepting, floating and letting time pass. And remember, when we learn to walk and live *with* fear, we eventually walk and live *without* fear.

THE RECORDINGS

Dr Weekes gives further help on CD and DVD for sufferers from nervous illness. The CDs are called:

Hope and Help for Your Nerves
Good Night, Good Morning
Nervous Fatigue
Moving to Freedom
Pass Through Panic

And the DVD is called:
Peace from Nervous Suffering

The recordings are available from:
Claire Weekes Publications Pty Ltd
PO Box 377
Woden ACT 2606
Australia

The DVDs are available from:
Pacific Recordings
32 Woodside Drive
Cottingley, Bingley
West Yorkshire BD16 1RF
United Kingdom

Visit claireweekes.com.au